Praise for *Little Kids, Big Worries: Stress-Busting Tips for Early Childhood Classrooms*

"Anything Alice Honig writes is a treasure, and this book is no exception."

—Bettye M. Caldwell, Ph.D.,
Professor Emerita, University of Arkansas at Little Rock

"Finally, an authoritative resource that offers parents and professionals a wealth of information about how to recognize signs of stress in the lives of young children, and more importantly, practical suggestions for what to do about it."

—Virginia Buysse, Ph.D.
Senior Scientist, FPG Child Development Institute,
University of North Carolina at Chapel Hill

"Amazingly practical advice on understanding how family, school and public events and relationships influence children's behavior. The stress-reducing strategies will really benefit both children and the adults who care for and teach them."

—Edna Runnels Ranck, Ed.D.,
President, OMEP-USA, The World Organization
for Early Childhood Education, Washington, D.C.

"Offers very helpful resources to teachers including a framework for recognizing, understanding, and supporting children displaying stress in the classroom."

—Richard G. Lambert, Ph.D., Ed.S.,
Professor, University of North Carolina, Charlotte

"Strikes the perfect balance between reducing stress and protecting children from harm while also promoting their coping skills and resilience. This powerful book is packed with practical strategies for teachers."

—Sue Bredekamp, Ph.D.,
Early Childhood Education Consultant

"This highly respected scholar presents a valuable anti̶d̶ rent academic emphasis in early educatio child approach, she provides practitione reduce young children's stress which we children's optimal education."

—......., Ph.D.,
Sterling Professor of Psychology, Emeritus, Yale University;
Director, Emeritus, The Edward Zigler Center in Child
Development and Social Policy; Former Chief, U.S. Children's Bureau

little kids
BIG WORRIES

STRESS-BUSTING TIPS
FOR EARLY CHILDHOOD CLASSROOMS

little kids
BIG WORRIES

STRESS-BUSTING TIPS
FOR EARLY CHILDHOOD CLASSROOMS

by

Alice Sterling Honig, Ph.D.
Professor Emerita of Child Development
Syracuse University
Syracuse, New York

·P·A·U·L·H·
BROOKES
PUBLISHING CO.®

Baltimore • London • Sydney

Paul H. Brookes Publishing Co.
Post Office Box 10624
Baltimore, Maryland 21285-0624
USA

www.brookespublishing.com

"Paul H. Brookes Publishing Co." is a registered trademark of
Paul H. Brookes Publishing Co., Inc.

Typeset by Broad Books, Baltimore, Maryland.
Manufactured in the United States of America by
Versa Press, Inc., East Peoria, Illinois.

The individuals described in this book are composites of real people whose situations have been masked and are based on the author's experiences. Names and identifying details have been changed to protect confidentiality.

The photos in this book that were provided by parents/guardians are used by permission of the individuals pictured and/or their parents/guardians.

Library of Congress Cataloging-in-Publication Data
Honig, Alice S.
  Little kids, big worries : stress-busting tips for early childhood classrooms / by Alice Sterling Honig
    p. cm.
  Includes bibliographical references and index.
  ISBN-13: 978-1-59857-061-8 (pbk.)
  ISBN-10: 1-59857-061-7 (pbk.)
  1. Early childhood education. 2. Stress in children—Prevention. 3. Classroom
  environment. I. Title.
  LB1139.23.H65 2010
  372.18'1—dc22   2009034139

British Library Cataloguing in Publication data are available from the British Library.

2013 2012 2011 2010 2009

10   9   8   7   6   5   4   3   2   1

CONTENTS

ABOUT THE AUTHOR

Alice Sterling Honig, Ph.D., is Professor Emerita of Child Development at Syracuse University in Syracuse, New York. Dr. Honig attended Cornell University, received her B.A. degree from Barnard College, her M.S. degree in experimental psychology from Columbia University, and her Ph.D. from Syracuse University in Developmental Psychology. For more than 40 years, Dr. Honig has taught courses in child development; parenting; cross-cultural study of children and families; language and cognitive development; quality caregiving with infants and toddlers; theories of child development; research issues and problems in child development; child observation and measurement techniques; prosocial and moral development; an Erikson seminar; and exemplary child enrichment programs. Every spring, for over 33 years, Dr. Honig has directed the National Quality Infant/Toddler Caregiving Workshop. She has authored or edited more than two dozen books and 500 articles and chapters.

A special Early Childhood Lifetime Achievement Award was presented in 2004 to Dr. Honig by the Syracuse Association for the Education of Young Children. The New York State Association for the Education of Young Children in 2005 gave Dr. Honig its "Champion of Children Lifetime Achievement Award." Dr. Honig was honored in 2008 with the Central New York State Psychological Association's Annual award given: "In Recognition of Outstanding Lifetime Contribution and Service." For over a decade, Dr. Honig co-conducted workshops for The Onondaga County Mental Health Association to help parents with child custody issues. As a licensed New York State psychologist, she counsels parents and assesses children's development. She is a contributing columnist for *Scholastic Parent and Child,* is North American Editor for the British journal *Early Child Development and Care,* and has served on many editorial boards, including the *American Journal of Orthopsychiatry, Child Development,* and *PsycCritiques.*

ACKNOWLEDGMENTS

Most of us in the field of child development owe so much to our mentors and to the projects in which we have been privileged to do research and to serve children and families. I am eternally grateful for the privilege that Dr. Bettye Caldwell offered me in working with her as she began her pioneer project to serve and enrich the lives of low-income infants in the early 1960s at the Children's Center in Syracuse, New York. I feel so fortunate for the lifelong friendship of care providers and child development outreach workers that became possible, as that project expanded years later (under the directorship of Dr. J.R. Lally) into the Family Development Research program, for which I served as Program Director. I have learned also from work with families in other cultures. For many decades, work with graduate students on research in many nations—such as Singapore, Taiwan, Turkey, France, and Korea—has deepened my appreciation of the complexity and wisdom of parenting in other cultures. I would like to express loving appreciation to my life partner, Dr. Arthur Komar, for his support and presence when I lectured and carried out research and consultations abroad in France and elsewhere, as these opportunities deeply enriched my knowledge and professional career. Finally, I would like to express special words of appreciation to the editorial and production team at Paul H. Brookes Publishing Co. Their harmonious helpfulness and professional expertise have been consistent and essential in bringing this book to fruition.

This book is dedicated in gratitude to my three children—Lawrence Sterling Honig, Madeleine Honig Lenski, and Jonathan David Honig—who, as loving parents of my grandchildren, have deepened my appreciation for, insights into, and delight in helping children flourish.

CHAPTER 1

UNDERSTANDING STRESS IN CHILDREN'S LIVES

Teachers are well aware that children, young as they are, may well have emotional troubles and mental health issues. Teachers witness strong angry outbursts, signs of fears and phobias, and defiant behaviors that signal sorrowful stressors in a child's life. Many stresses exist for children in our rushed and technologically complex society. Some children have continuing health issues, such as chronic asthma or illness. Some are acutely worried about school issues, such as bullying or struggling with learning problems that leave a lasting legacy of worry. Losses are a sorrowful source of stress in children's lives. In today's world, stresses from a family member's death may be rare, but stresses from abandonment by a well-loved family member occur; for example, a child loses contact with a parent who feels it is too painful to maintain family contact after a difficult divorce. Even some daily hassles, such as when a substitute caregiver arrives and a cautious child feels quite upset, present us with the challenge of how we can ease a child's distress.

Stress is currently such a prominent concern for parents and providers that web sites now offer daily advice for handling stress. The Child Care Lounge e-mail site (2006) posted its reasons for addressing stress issues:

> I think we like to visualize childhood as a time that is carefree and inno-
> cent. The truth is young children are not always isolated or immune to
> trauma and day-to-day stress. Some stress is normal but more and more
> children are impacted by it. (p. 1)

Children's cartoons are even taking note that toddlers may be affected by stress, as in the cartoon featuring the infant Marvin. A young toddler friend, sitting with Marvin in a baby wading pool, communicates (by cartoon bubble!) that he is already feeling under "an extraordinary amount of pressure"!

Adults who face mild daily hassles or more acute stresses fortunately possess a large repertoire of coping techniques. Adults use cognitive skills to plan ahead to avoid stress. They make alternate plans. When snarled traffic blocks the usual highway to their job, most adults do not go into road-rage mode. They figure out how to get off the highway and take an alternate route so that they can get to work on time. Teachers who recognize worrisome stresses in a child are good detectives and good thinkers. They use a variety of strategies to galvanize assistance, such as alerting the administrator and consulting with the school counselor.

Young children, in contrast, are just beginning to develop the thinking and emotional skills that permit them to adjust to unexpected changes. Even small changes are hard for young children. Parents might be puzzled about why a baby, who has experienced a change in providers every few months, is acting cranky and obstinate every morning. They feel exasperated. Why can't he just accept these changes the family felt that they had to make? The crying child who fusses about being left at the new place is expressing inner stress and a lack of ability to cope with these changes. He is using the only tool he has to communicate stress: upset crying. Parental understanding will help. Caregivers' gentle persistence in winning a young child's basic trust (Erikson, 1950) will be of crucial help.

DEFINING STRESS

What is stress? Why do we need to be concerned about stressors in the lives of children and their child care providers? *Stress* is when a person shows, by difficulties in personal relationships and worrisome bodily responses, that he or she is having a struggle and cannot cope with felt or perceived difficulties (Honig, 1986a). Selye (1982), the father of stress research, defined *stress* more specifically as a stimulus event that is severe enough to produce disequilibrium in the homeostatic physiological systems.

Sources of stress abound. They arise from biological or medical risks (e.g., prematurity, cerebral palsy), personal or social factors (e.g., lack of warm, responsive parenting), family circumstances (e.g., maternal depression, lack of father support for mother), and sociodemographic factors (e.g., living in a dangerous neighborhood with bullets flying from gang fights) (Honig, 1986b). Child stresses have long-lasting negative consequences. Stresses from personal interactions, such as persistent peer rejection, isolation, and peer bullying, cause severe and lasting stress and developmental difficulties from ages 5 to 12 (Ladd, 2006; Lines, 2008; Zins, Elias, & Maher, 2007).

Studies over many decades of infants born at risk on the island of Kauai (Werner & Smith, 1992) revealed that those adults who grew up *resilient* had experienced a loving relationship as babies with their moms during the first year and a close consistent relationship with her during early childhood. Relationships with loving, intimate persons are crucial for preventing stress and for ameliorating risk factors that stress young children. This book provides many vignettes and personal examples of how children express stress and how insightful and caring teachers can alleviate those stresses.

CHILDREN'S BEHAVIORS REVEAL STRESS IN THEIR LIVES

We need to watch children's body language as well as listen to their words to become more aware of stress. Body responses are helpful signposts. They confirm emotional vulnerabilities and inner distress even when young children are not able to tell us in words. How do children's bodies and behavior show us their distress? A child's eyes widen and the brow wrinkles with worry lines. A baby who is usually bouncy has limbs that feel floppy or stiff and rigid. A child chews and sucks on the ends of her hair as she sits at her desk in school with hunched over shoulders. A young child's eyes are dull or angry looking. The child's face is unsmiling (Koplow, 1996). A child's jaw aches from grinding teeth at naptime. Frequent constipation or diarrhea without any medical reason can indicate stress. Some children earnestly report a terrible tummyache that miraculously disappears if a parent says the child can

Table 1.1   Child Stress: Behaviors and body signals

Are the young children in your care thriving emotionally? Perceptive awareness and monitoring of baby and toddler behaviors is your first line of defense against emotional troubles. The following body cues, especially when you see several in the same child, indicate that the child's mental health may be in jeopardy.

Dull, unsparkling eyes
Back arching and body stiffening as a regular response
Avoidance of eye contact
Pushing away from rather than relaxed body molding to the caregiver
Limp, floppy, listless body
Rare smiles despite tender adult elicitation
Compulsive body rocking, thumb sucking, self-stimulation
Inconsolable crying for long periods
Scattered attention during intimate exchanges with caregiver
Apathetic facial expression
Lack of empathy—impassiveness or anger when a peer is hurt or distressed
Lack of responsiveness to warm adult overtures
Long and frequent temper tantrums
Fearful withdrawal or flinching from caregiver's caress
Anxious shadowing of or clinging to provider even after months in care
Regular avoidance of or indifference to parents at pickup time
Continuous biting or hitting of others without provocation
Little or no interest in peers or others
Grimaces of despair
Going too easily between adults with no sign that any one caregiver is special
Persistent head banging against crib
Tendency to run off, heedless of the caregiver's presence as a safe base
Aimless wandering; inability to focus or settle into constructive play
Reckless actions that endanger the child; lack of awareness of body limits
Overly anxious or overly compliant with adults
Oversolicitousness toward adults—parentification

If you observe a child showing clusters of the behaviors listed above, work with family members to alleviate the child's stress. In some cases you may need to help families connect with community resources to support the emotionally distressed child.

Adapted, with permission, from Honig, A.S. "Mental Health for Babies: What Do Theory and Research Teach Us?" *Young Children* 48 (March 1993), 72. [As adapted in A.S. Honig, *Secure Relationships: Nurturing Infant/Toddler Attachment in Early Care Settings,* (Washington, DC: NAEYC, 2002), 33.]

then stay home from school. Some children do not say anything defiant or angry but avoid eye contact persistently and give adults sullen looks whenever asked to do something. A child whose parent is away at war may act far more subdued and clingy with the parent left at home. Table 1.1 provides a list of some telltale signs of stress in young children (Honig, 1986b, p. 160).

SIGNS OF STRESS VARY
IN INTENSITY AND DURATION

Some stress reactions are brief. Others last a long while. Stress behaviors can be disturbingly dramatic. Evie pulls out clumps of her own hair (trichotillomania) and leaves large bald spots on her head. Barrie bursts into lengthy, terrifying temper tantrums; he holds his breath and almost turns blue when told he cannot have a candy so temptingly displayed near the supermarket checkout counter. Jeremy becomes furiously angry and screams at another child, whom he perceives as interfering with his play activity.

> Jamal was building a tower of large plastic blocks. Sitting nearby and watching the tower going up, Bettina tried helpfully to steady a wobbly block that Jamal had plunked down without adjusting its balance on top of the block below. Jamal smacked her hand away, frowned, and screamed at this helpful gesture, as if Bettina were trying to interfere and even perhaps deprive him of his own building activity. She withdrew her hand and looked worried. Jamal continued building his wobbly tower.

Not all children show us their inner stress by overt behaviors. Some manifest subtler ways of showing that adults are overpowering or intrusive in their lives. Negativism is sometimes developmentally appropriate, and sometimes it is a sign of distress. Toddlers learning to say *no* are asserting their newly growing feelings of competence and independence. They are right on target developmentally.

> "Larry, it is time for lunch," called out Ms. Ali. Bright eyed, Larry ran to the other end of the room, calling out "No, no, no." Then he turned and gave his caregiver a dazzling smile as if she too should share in his delight at being able to express his own independence. She smiled and remarked, "Mmm, yummy meat; yummy carrots!" and the toddler happily ran over to his high chair.

However, some preschoolers and school-age children say *no* a lot even to reasonable and cheerful adult requests. This may be a sign that a child feels he or she must defend himself against feelings of too many adult pressures or conflicting adult orders. Teachers who want to gain insights into how children are sometimes buffeted by too many adult orders can listen in public spaces to family talk that reveals the source of some children's conflicted feelings of being ordered about too much. Here is one such conversation overheard:

After eating his meal, 6-year-old Donny had taken off his shoes in anticipation of enjoying the children's section of the fast-food restaurant, where he could play on the enclosed climbers. "Come here, your shirt is crooked," called his father. Donny frowned and ran back to the table. His father adjusted the shirt, and then Donny trotted back to the play space. "Don't run," called his mother, "You will fall!" "Careful climbing, do you hear me?" ordered his father. "Come here. I want to check your socks," Mom called. Donny ran back and forth, trying to be obedient. His brows were knit, and his face looked sober and upset. He felt like a puppet being jerked on a string.

HOW ADULTS HANDLE A CHILD'S STRESS

Suppose a child confides that the grown-ups in the family always decide for her but never ask her what she wants when they are bringing her for child care to one relative or another. "I really want to be with my Grandpa when they are going out, but my parents never ask me about *my* feelings," the child confides to a sympathetic teacher in a discouraged tone. How should the adult respond? One teacher may listen quietly; another teacher confirms verbally the child's longing that grown-ups ask her more about her wishes. A teacher could also ask the child care center's director to invite the parents in for a friendly talk about how well the child is getting along at the center as well as the relationships at home that seem to make her feel really happy.

Adults call children stubborn or uncooperative when they defend their needs against too much adult pressure. Baby Billy holds food in his check pouches and refuses the spoon with tightly pursed lips when he feels that he is being fed too fast or too much.

Teachers become aware of how children defend their autonomy by saying *no* in the classroom well beyond their toddler years. Insightful teachers find ways to empower a young child, whose response to feeling thwarted or helpless in the face of perceived overwhelming and sometimes arbitrary adult power is to act stubborn.

Different parenting styles are associated with different behavioral outcomes. When children feel under too much pressure from authoritarian parents, they may be compliant and obedient at home but act out aggressively and noncompliantly in the classroom. Baumrind (1971) noted three major types of parenting in her research. *Authoritarian parents* are not warm. They value control and unquestioning obedience to rules. They punish children forcefully for violating their rules. Their attitude of "Do as I say because I am your parent" proclaims that they have all the rights; children have all the responsibilities. Their children tend to be more distrustful. *Permissive parents* are warm, noncontrolling, and make few demands on children. Their children tend to be more immature and the least self-controlled. *Authoritative parents* have high expectations, act loving and accepting, show genuine personalized interest in their children, and explain rules and expectations that they require. Their preschoolers tend to be the most self-reliant, contented, and self-controlled. Children who show strong upset in mild encounters with peers or strong negativism well into the preschool years may be experiencing less effective rearing styles at home.

> Howie, 5 years old, often says that he is not hungry and does not want lunch. His kindly provider is puzzled when he strongly refuses her offers of his favorite foods. She notices perceptively that he acts quite cranky from hunger just prior to lunchtime. The provider does not force or nag him. However, when the others are already eating and he sees a food he really does like, then he suddenly and urgently demands that food. His teacher also notices that his interactions with the other children in the classroom are far more cheerful after he has eaten.

Caregivers do need to know many techniques and ways to handle child stress in order to nurture more positive developmental outcomes. But the first helping step is to enhance awareness of the myriad ways in which stress manifests itself in young children. It is easy to recognize that a child in a temper tantrum is upset. We also need to tune in to the many other ways children tell us about inner distress. Florence has to wait after her center closes for a driver to pick her up and take her to a sitter for a few hours, because her parents have long working hours that extend beyond the time that the center operates. Adults supervise her safe transfer. Florence bites her lips nervously and says that she has to "go pee" every few minutes while waiting for the transfer. This transfer is a daily procedure, but it nevertheless stresses this child.

TEACHERS AND STRESS

What about stress in teacher's lives? Stresses occur in everyone's life, including the personal lives of care providers. Stresses occur among staff members, or between a caregiver and a parent, in addition to adult frustrations when children behave in puzzling or inappropriate ways. So endemic is stress in society that if we look at web sites and daily e-mails, every day brings a message of how adults can reduce their stress and what products they can purchase, from aromatherapy bath products to advertisements for yoga lessons! Colleges are addressing stress issues among students and offering courses to combat stress. One such course is called Mindfulness-Based Stress Reduction (MBSR) to teach young adults faced with life stresses to practice "open, nonjudgmental awareness of the present moment, by dealing in a more balanced way with what arrives" (Syracuse University, 2006, p. 7). The last two chapters of this book provide ideas for decreasing stress in the lives of child care providers and teachers and provide ideas about when to and how to utilize outside help such as mental health professionals.

SHORT-TERM STRESSORS

Short-term stress is not always negative. Actually, a *moderate* amount of stress alerts a person, enhances memory, and heightens the chance to forge ahead in thinking of ways to improve the stressful situation. Stress has been conceptualized by the head of the neuroendocrinology laboratory at Rockefeller University as a positive experience if a person has a feeling of control and satisfaction. That person faces and accepts a challenge that he or she is determined to struggle to overcome (McEwen, 2002).

A teacher on vacation is determined to walk most of the Appalachian Trail over a few weeks of vacation time. The trail is often difficult and has discomforts. But at the end of the trip the teacher feels victorious and exhilarated.

Even for children, mild stresses can actually lead to joy and feelings of competence when their efforts to overcome the stress are successful.

An older toddler, frustrated with struggling hard to learn to whistle for weeks, suddenly succeeded! Early one morning, he stood up and held on to the bars of his crib, which was in his parents' bedroom. Crowing with triumph and waking his startled parents, he called out "I dooed it; I dooed it!" and produced a recognizable whistling sound.

A kindergartener had been worrying for weeks in class. He kept trying to figure out how to recognize and find a rhyme after the teacher had taught that *words that rhyme end in the same sound.* Although he felt frustrated, he worked hard with his teacher's gentle and positive encouragement. A few weeks later, when she asked the children, "Tell me a part of your face that rhymes with *rose*," he grinned with joy and called out "nose!" This learning challenge was mildly stressful, but it galvanized him to try and succeed. And he did!

Some situations that have been regarded as very difficult or stressful for children really do not have adverse consequences. Research at the University of Maryland has shown that busy schedules for children with music or ballet lessons, sports activities, play dates, and so forth are not by themselves stressful. The children reacted negatively not to busy schedules but indeed felt stressed by parental criticisms and severe pressures to excel (St. George, 2008).

Are short-term stresses easier to cope with? Some short-term stresses are mild, such as a child's forgetting to take his homework back to school on the day it is due and getting scolded by the teacher. Even mild stresses may cause temporary troubles. A mild stress, such as moving a preschooler to a new room to make her room into a nursery for the new baby to be born, may disappear fairly quickly. Some adults are quite adept at anticipating any such stress before it discomforts the child too much. They provide calm, loving explanations. They enlist the child to help redecorate the new room to which she or he is being moved. They make the child feel proud of growing up so that the coming change seems a positive rather than a worrisome event to anticipate. But adults have to think about a stressor in terms of *how the child views the event* rather than from an adult perspective. For example, a stress that might seem mild to adults but may cause sorrow for a child occurs when the family of his best friend next door moves far away. When young children in group care are moved to the next older classroom together with their friends, then stress is decreased. Yet a center often has rigid rules to move children at certain ages, or when they become mobile, from one group care room to the next.

Although time limited, even a one-time severe stress can have lingering effects. Suppose a teacher or child suddenly falls quite ill while in the classroom, and a sensitive preschooler sobs in terror. An angry child hurls a toy, hits another child, and causes bleeding. A stress may be acute, such as when a toddler screams as a dog on the street jumps on him. But this intensely fearful episode may have long-term consequences. The teacher notices for weeks afterward that this child withdraws fearfully and will not even go near the cage with a small, gentle gerbil.

LONG-TERM STRESSORS

Some stresses are long term. Long-term stress occurs when a person feels he or she does not have the capability to resolve the stress or control the stressful situation. The consequences are biologically harmful. During such stressful situations our bodies release adrenaline, which speeds up heart rate, increases blood pressure, and prepares our bodies for emergency actions. Poverty is a long-term stressor for many children. In the United States, more than 13 million children live in families with incomes below the federal poverty level of $21,200 annual income. Poverty stresses parents. Family poverty increases child stress when parents lack resources and energy to supply the quintessential love and cherishing that children need (Cauthen & Fass, 2008).

Long-term stressors for children may be *indirect* rather than direct. A child with recurring cancer is hospitalized frequently. His siblings feel worried and neglected. They express resentment that their parents are busy with the needs of the very ill child and often not emotionally available for them. In addition, they feel guilty, because they realize how sick the sibling is. Another child moves from one crowded shelter to another with his homeless mother and siblings. He suddenly has to change schools. Worry, bewilderment, and stress are pervasive for this child.

Divorce

Divorce is a frequent stressor for young children. In some cases, divorce does bring to an end the ongoing fights and tension that have worried a child. But in many cases, divorce has proved a long-term stressor. Some parents fight bitterly for custody of a child; they hurl contempt-filled and hurtful accusations about one another to the children. The children start to fight a lot with each other and with friends. Therapists and researchers observe that in families experiencing these hardships, the long-term stressors from acrimonious divorce and custody battles result in a child's plummeting grades, sadness, fights with peers on the playground, bedwetting, and even nightmares and interpersonal sorrows later in adult life (Marquardt, 2005; Wallerstein, 1987; Wallerstein, Lewis, & Blakeslee, 2000). Ongoing parental feuds and hatreds after divorce can affect preschool staff as well as the child. A handsome 3-year-old, loved by each parent, confided sadly to his preschool teacher, "Nobody is my friend." He felt so lonely in the class. His parents were continuing their bitter divorce fight for years afterward, and each tried to enlist the teachers into taking sides in their psychological battles.

Some time-limited stressors still feel traumatic to children already beset by the stress of divorce. A stepfather's new wife has a baby, and a child worries that she will not be loved as much as the new baby they are doting upon. Or she fears that there will no longer be room for her to sleep at their home. A mother's boyfriend is babysitting and inappropriately sexually touches the young child, saying that this is their secret. The child begins to acts nervous and shrinks from her teacher's touch in the classroom (Gordon, 1983).

Dislocations and Relocations

Dislocations and relocations of living sites are scary for children. In war zones, children flee into crowded refugee camps. Their grave faces and clinging ways speak volumes about inner stress. Even when a refugee or immigrant family finds safe refuge in a new country with a different language, a child's emotional distress from dislocation in space and in culture may last over a longer period of time.

For children in military families whose parents are often deployed overseas, relocation can be a significant source of stress. The children are faced with the sudden departure of a parent whom they worry is going off to a dangerous place. The parent's new assignment may be a locale that their children may have seen portrayed on television as a place with bombings and killing. Relocation during times of peace can be likewise stressful for these children. They move to a new apartment in a new town and have no friends at first in a new school. Such relocations can cause heartache and worry. Children may exhibit acting out behaviors such as bedwetting, bullying, or other telltale signals of distress.

Garbarino (2008) has illuminated with striking examples from across the world the stresses that children experience living in difficult circumstances, such as social conditions of fear and brutality, exposure to war and terror, or life in displaced-persons camps. He reminds us that unless we care enough to ameliorate stresses in children's lives everywhere, the later consequences for children can be sad and atrocious, such as youth-group violence, teen prostitution, drug abuse, and the perpetuation of violence in future generations.

Abandonment: The Strongest Source of Stress for Children

Grief at death or loss of a child's beloved parent or close sibling often brings forth depressive child symptoms. Strong fears of further abandonment impel worrisome child behaviors. They imperil school learning and cause overly cautious behaviors (Bowlby, 2000).

> Ashley, a 5-year-old, was behaving "super good" all the time. The mother smugly remarked on what a good child she had. The family therapist quietly asked the mother to think about the fact that she had willingly agreed to give the other parent custody of the older sibling. The extremely well-behaved little girl was acting on her secret worries. If Ashley were not always a good child, then maybe Mommy too would disappear from her life, just as Daddy and her older sister had done.

Such fears can mark a child with stress over many years.

SEVERE STRESS AND BRAIN CHANGES IN CHILDREN

When stress is chronic and unrelieved during the early years of life, not only a child's personality and behaviors but also the brain undergo harmful effects. When the body is overexposed to cortisol, adrenaline, norepinephrine, and other stress chemicals, brain cells are damaged. Raised levels of stress hormones cause the hippocampus, the brain's moderator of memories, to atrophy. Dr. Bruce Perry (1999), a child psychiatrist who has treated thousands of children who have been neglected and abused, underscored the gravity of atrophy of the hippocampus—the seat of memory. Children, who need all of their brain capacity for early learning, are at particular risk from long-term, chronic stressors such as family violence. Loving, intimately nurturing caregivers are the first line of defense against overwhelming child stressors of neglect and abuse. Dr. Perry (2002) has been explicit on how harmful the effects of severe stressors can be on a child's developing brain.

> Children need to have both stable emotional attachments with and touch from primary adult caregivers, and spontaneous interactions with peers. If these connections are lacking, brain development both of caring behavior and cognitive capacities is damaged in a lasting fashion. The impacts of technology have spawned declines in extended families, family meals, and spontaneous peer interactions. The latter changes have deprived many children of experiences that promote positive growth of the cognitive and caring potentials of their developing brains. (p. 79)

Perry (1994) categorized parental neglect as a damaging *catastrophe,* a long-lasting child stress that causes negative changes in brain patterns. Some children cannot even remember the pain they have undergone. They blank out early experiences. Michael, a star football player whose father had been murdered and whose mother was a crack addict, had lived in many foster homes. While in high school, college football teams courted him for his awesome football skills. He had learning difficulties and required intensive and massive daily doses of tutoring help. When his nurturing adoptive mother asked about his past, he could not respond. He had wiped out childhood memories as a way to cope with ever-present stresses in his past. "Michael spent his whole life as a problem to be covered up" (Lewis, 2006, p. 112).

STRESS NEGATIVELY AFFECTS CHILDREN'S BODY PHYSIOLOGY

The consequences of severe stress when they are prolonged and involved include many somatic symptoms. This syndrome is called *posttraumatic stress disorder* (PTSD). Some symptoms are chronic sleep interruptions, horrifying flashbacks in memory, sudden angers, and nonphysical bodily sensations that feel crippling, such as fiery arm aches or headaches. Dissociation, obsessive ruminations, or the opposite where memories of the traumatic happenings are wiped out are also typical in PTSD. About one third of soldiers returning from serving in the Iraq war are diagnosed with PTSD and in need of mental health services. Some children who have been assaulted or neglected suffer from signs of PTSD. They space out in the classroom and seemingly do not hear the teacher. In a therapy session they compulsively act out the trauma again and again. Right after the September 11, 2001, terror attacks, teachers reported that some preschoolers were setting up tall block towers and pretending to bomb them with toy airplanes until the blocks crashed down, over and over.

What does chronic severe stress do to a body? During a stressful event, the adrenal gland releases adrenaline. This accelerates the heart rate and increases breathing and blood pressure. Adrenaline alerts and prepares the body to fight or flee. The adrenal gland also releases cortisol. Cortisol goes to the brain to help lodge the stressful event in memory and also to keep the emergency response going. Norepinephrine "is the caveman fight-or-flight chemical. It's what tells you to tangle with a saber-toothed tiger or hightail it to safety out of your hut" (Roizen & Oz, 2006, p. 134). Usually, after a stressful event is over the body returns to normal. What happens when a child's body is under stress continually from severe daily criticism, threats, or physical punishments? The adrenal system remains active.

Chronic stress shortens caps, called *telomeres,* which are chunks of DNA at the ends of chromosomes. Stress shortens telomeres and leads to premature cell aging. Such shortening of telomeres was found in mothers who spent lengthy time caring for chronically ill children and who perceived themselves as highly stressed. Their white blood cells also showed more aging than other women the same age without such stress burdens (Cheney, 2006).

Severe stresses from chronic neglect or abuse cause the body to produce much higher levels of cortisol, adrenaline, and norepinephrine. Blood pressure is elevated and there is more chance for clogged arteries (atherosclerosis). Perry (1993) teaches that if an aggravated adult habitually scolds a child who has been abused or neglected, that child may show freeze, flight, or fight responses. A care provider might interpret the freezing response as the child ignoring her and paying no attention to what she has said. Caregivers need to be alert to the three responses described as typical consequences of child abuse or neglect stress.

A prison psychologist interviewed hundreds of convicted delinquent youth (Welsh, 1976). The youth gave detailed descriptions about parental discipline methods in their childhood. Independently, judges rated the severity of each of the criminal actions for which each youth was convicted. The more that parents had used severe physical punishment in childhood, the more severe were the delinquent actions the youth were convicted of, as rated by the independent judges.

Chaotic and hurtful childhoods lead to worrisome personality outcomes such as aggression and predatory violence in adulthood as well as drug abuse and victimization. These findings are widespread in many cultures. Researchers in New Zealand reported that poverty, witnessing violence at home, and bullying at school are significant risk factors for child depression (Denny, Clark, Fleming, & Wall, 2004).

Furthermore, some children, scolded and ridiculed for years, learn to distrust their own actions, judgments, and decisions. They have so frequently had the experience of negative consequences from family as a consequence of their actions. Plagued by low and unstable self-images, these children grow up to become gullible, duped by others, and victims of promotional scams, false advertising, and unscrupulous friends. They are apt to give false confessions and become followers of religious cults (Graceffo, 2006).

STRESSES HAVE MULTIPLICATIVE EFFECTS

Stresses in a child's life do not just add up; they multiply their worrisome effects. Rutter (1996), an English psychiatrist, suggested that there is a quadratic or threshold effect of stress. That is, after an individual reaches his or her stress threshold, there is a four-fold jump in developmental problems if more stresses are piled on a child. Researchers have investigated whether the *number of stressors* or the *variety of contexts* where stresses occur, such as school, home, or neighborhood, would affect children differently. For low-income elementary school children, context was not as important as number. Regardless of where they were stressed, the *cumulative number of stressors* provoked more negative child outcomes (Morales & Guerro, 2006). The researchers reported, "The accumulation of stressors, irrespective of their context, was related to small to moderate decreases in achievement, moderate increases in depression, and large increases in aggression" (p. 919).

PERCEPTION OF STRESSORS VARIES WITH INDIVIDUALS

Children differ in perception of threats from stressors. Although there are myriad sources of stress in children's lives, perception of stress varies among children. When a hungry and tired toddler is digging in with both hands while eating, even being sharply reminded at lunchtime to use a spoon can cause tension. Toilet learning causes fearful worries for some youngsters. Some toddlers fear being sucked down into a big toilet. If not allowed to use a small potty set safely on the floor, toilet learning is traumatic for them, and they may fiercely resist the most patient efforts.

Different kinds of stressors and how they are perceived *vary greatly with child developmental level.* Walking in the wintry dusk to the supermarket parking lot with a baby in arms, a mom stiffens in terror when an armed felon accosts her. However, the baby may even smile upon seeing the funny gesticulations and waving gun that the felon is pointing! Yet a few years later that same child will sob and scream if such an attack occurs.

Gender and Stress

Some stressors affect boys and girls differently. Very young males, compared with females, show more vulnerability to deprivation of maternal warmth (Martin, 1981). First-grade teachers rated boys with an extensive history of child care as more disobedient, quarrelsome, and uncooperative than children without such a history (Robertson, 1982). Howes (1999) pointed out that the quality of home care as well as child care may well affect such findings. Yet researchers have found that boys have a greater risk of difficulties in social adjustment, compared with girls, after many years of nonfamilial child care (National Institute of Child Health and Human Development–Early Childhood Care Research Network [ECCRN], 2001, 2006).

Gender effects showed up in a study of Israeli classrooms for 4-year-olds who had already been in child care for a considerable period of time. In this nonrisk sample of preschoolers, some of the classes had a higher ratio of teachers per child and others had fewer teachers per child (Bornstein, Hahn, Gist, & Haynes, 2006). When there were fewer adults for the group, the boys proved far more emotionally vulnerable than the girls. Their teachers reported that those boys exhibited "more externalizing and internalizing problems, which are characterized generally by lower attentional regulation, inhibitory control, and delay of gratification as well as higher impulsivity, and which include symptoms of anxiety and depression" (p. 147). The girls' behaviors did not reveal these worrisome outcomes whether they experienced fewer or more caregivers in their child care group. Head Start boys, but not girls, were more likely to act hostile and aggressive if there was teacher–child conflict (Ewing & Taylor, 2009). In this study, only gender differences, but not ethnic differences, were related to child stress.

Directors will want to alert teachers to the emotional needs of little boys, and their need for nurturing interactions. Many adults have been taught that boys are stronger than girls and do not need as many loving cuddles. Caregivers need to realize how much young males need their nurturing care.

NOTICING STRESS: A SUBTLE ART

Teachers and care providers know that they have to be skilled in keeping young children safe and be able to prepare curricular experiences to motivate children to become zestful learners. Yet those individuals teaching and caring for children need to know a lot about children's emotional development and especially how to counteract the effects of stressors. Kicking, biting, screaming—these are easy to interpret as child stress responses. But many signs of child stress are subtler. A teacher told me that during the past year she had a student who daydreamed, looking out of the window rather than paying attention in class. The teacher had made many sarcastic comments to the girl. At the end of the year she found out that the girl was being pressured into an untenable sexual situation at home and felt that she had nobody to talk to. Before assuming a school-age child is not cooperating in class, adults need to think of secret or not-so-secret stresses that may be influencing that child's behaviors.

An important illustration of how differently children perceive stress was revealed in the variety of mental health outcomes reported among children of the London Blitz during the Second World War, when German V-2 rockets obliterated parts of London. Many families sent their children to live with strangers in the countryside so that the children would be safe from the bombs. Families whose children remained with them hurried down to the deep underground train platforms as soon as the sirens screamed their warnings of an imminent bombing attack. The children sent away were found to suffer more bedwetting and nightmares. Stresses were less and mental health better for those children who had to go to sleep lying on the cold subway station floor but close to a loved parent or neighbor. The presence of loving, well-known adults proved a mediating bulwark for children against the terrors and stresses of the Nazi Blitz. Children may *perceive* life difficulties differently, but caring adults remain the precious persons who can create and provide mitigating factors to decrease stress.

Different ways of perceiving stress as devastation or opportunity can be found among adults too. Suppose a person loses a job, takes that opportunity to get an educational grant, goes for further training, and then finds a much more satisfying position. A different person losing a job might be confronted by an angry spouse, feel bitter and ashamed, worry over how to pay bills, and start drinking heavily.

Some changes in life are viewed as stressful even when positive, such as the excitement (and burden) of preparing for a big family get-together at the holiday season. Perception is critical. Do we view a change or a stressful happening as something to shrug off, as an interesting challenge, something we can live through, or do we perceive it as scary, infuriating, and acutely upsetting?

Overwhelming stresses, such as torture, are terrible for *all* people. However, children differ in how they perceive ordinary life stresses, whether milder or more troublesome, in their lives.

VARIATIONS IN RESPONSE TO STRESS

People respond in various ways to life stresses. Children differ not only in their perceptions of stress but also in the *resiliency* of their responses to stress (Honig, 1986a, 1986b, 2009).

Some teachers might think that child disability would invariably impair a child's responses to stress. Yet some typically developing children might be more vulnerable in their capacity to cope with stress compared with a child born with or incurring a later disability. Robert Louis Stevenson, the poet and author of *A Child's Garden of Verses* (Stevenson, 1924), was born quite sickly. His parents, busy with their adult social lives, left him in the care of a Scottish nursemaid who told him many tales. Although chronically sick, he read omnivorously and grew up to become a famous author.

In a fifth-grade classroom, one of the students complimented James, a blind student, on how well he was learning Spanish compared with the other students. She asked why he was so skillful at learning the language compared to his classmates. "Use your ears, girl, use your ears!" the student boomed out jovially in reply. James had learned to compensate for lack of vision by superbly honing his auditory skills to become a successful language student.

School-age children respond in many of the same and in many different ways to emotional troubles. Some children are stressed by being *overprogrammed;* they feel too hurried in life (Elkind, 1981). Some fight. Some steal. A little girl felt neglected emotionally by her father who was always out of the home ministering to families in difficulties. She stole a watch from another girl on a play date at one home. An adult needs to think deeply about the symbolism of the stressful behavior. What does stealing symbolize? "In some cases, the stolen items seem to symbolize a parent's love, power, or authority, of which the child feels deprived" (Papalia & Olds, 1995, p. 331). Desperate to feel more important, to feel more powerful, and to gain more friends, some children tell whopping lies to impress peers. "My uncle is going to give me a pony for Christmas," boasted a 6-year-old to his kindergarten classmates. He rarely saw his mother's brother, who was unemployed at the time.

When children continue to make up fanciful boasts or tell tall tales well into the elementary school years, teachers need to be aware that these tall tales are signals of insecurity. Some children whine a great deal. Others develop school phobias and refuse to go to school. One boy, whose well-educated, loving parents fought often and loudly, refused to go to school for months. His behavior signaled his strong anxious feeling that if only he were home all the time, then maybe he could make sure his parents were all right together.

Deeply afraid of the dark, a child may demand not only a night light but also a fully lighted room to go to sleep. Another child shows strong separation anxiety as he shadows the caregiver; he clings to her clothing for months. Talking with his dad, the teacher finds out that the child had watched a traumatic event—his pet dog had been run over and killed by a car.

Freudian Defense Mechanisms in Response to Stress

Dr. Freud (1935) explained that we all use special techniques once in a while to ward off anxious feelings. These Freudian defense mechanisms are used commonly to decrease tension, avoid criticism, and feel calmer. Suppose a visiting family member criticizes our housekeeping. Rather than accepting the critical comment philosophically as sometimes true of our housekeeping style, even as adults we react in stressed ways. Feeling angry, we are tempted to lash out *defensively* to cope with our anxious feelings. We may then return an accusation against the accuser as being sloppy too, or not the greatest at parenting! One 7-year-old whose very strict mother called her a "bad girl" retorted, "*You're* a bad girl!"

Some children use a more worrisome defense mechanism: *denial.* They say they did not break the item they just broke or hit the child they just slugged. A child might accusingly say that another child did it, "not me!" Blaming others is a defense mechanism called *projection of evil.* When I was a child, my mom read me a story called *Bad Mousie* (Dudley, 1947). The pictures show a little girl whose mouse friend, she claims, is always doing naughty things. He threw all of Donnie's clean socks into the bathtub when it had water in it. He tipped over orange juice and spilled cocoa. The little girl was told not to touch stuff on Mama's dresser. Her mother comes into her bedroom and finds perfume spilled all over the floor; Mama finds pots piled up into a tower and crashed all over the floor. She asks what happened. Each time, the little girl earnestly replies that Bad Mousie (rather than herself) has done the naughty deed. Mama tries to send Bad Mousie away, but he always comes back and is naughty once more. Near the end of the story, the little girl teaches him to be neat and careful with stuff and they all live happily together—a convenient fairy tale ending, but not so easy to accomplish in the real world.

Some children use the defense mechanism of *displacement.* If a teacher or parent yells at them, they then turn and fight with a sibling or peer, or kick the dog, as in Viorst's (1976) story *Alexander and the Terrible, Horrible, No Good, Very Bad Day.* In this story, Mom's bad feelings because Dad forgot to give mom a loving good-bye in the morning escalate and spill onto her grumpiness with each child, and in turn each acts upset with a younger sibling, and finally the dog gets the brunt of the grumpiness!

When parents use the mechanism of *displacement* (Ayoub, Grace, & Newberger, 1990), the abused child is often the target of displaced anger that breeds in the family:

> The child may indeed become a scapegoat for many family problems; he or she thus allows parents to avoid marital difficulties or other family conflicts. . . . Negative messages may be relayed to the child directly or indirectly. Indirect messages can leave the child with no way to respond. For example, a parent repeatedly says, "Good children never wet their beds," to a child who is a bed wetter. When the child wets his bed, the parent says nothing, but sighs deeply. (p. 235)

We need to learn to recognize a great many Freudian defense mechanisms as they play out in behaviors among children. Asked why he had kicked a child on the playground during earlier recess at school, Jimmy looked up at the teacher and said, "I don't know what you are talking about." Jimmy did not often seem to be lying. But it did seem as if, in fright at being punished, he did *repress* unpleasant episodes. They were not available to his memory.

Regression is a defense mechanism that worried young children use. They might demand a baby bottle rather than a glass to drink from after the new baby is born. One kindergarten child soiled his underpants for weeks when a family move in the neighborhood forced him to walk a new and unfamiliar route to his school.

Some children use the mechanism of *sour grapes*. Kylie defiantly tells the teacher, "Anyway, I wouldn't even want to play with that stupid old baby toy" right after the teacher has just stopped him from grabbing the toy from another child. Psychological *splitting* occurs when a person endows one intimate other (e.g., the new wife) with all the good characteristics and another person (e.g., the former spouse) with all the bad characteristics. If a teacher has had a child from one family in a prior class, the teacher may remember that child as smart and well behaved. When a younger sibling, somewhat mischievous and not as good a student, arrives in that teacher's class, the younger child may be considered to be a bad child in contrast with the good child the teacher formerly had in class.

Information about the many *defense mechanisms* people use to decrease their own anxiety and stress is empowering. As adults we need to become more aware of when we ourselves are using one defense mechanism or another to protect against feelings of distress. A gentle teacher, Ms. Rosie saw Alex suddenly raise his arm and hit Robbie with a block quite hard on the head. Robbie had been standing close by and looking on with great interest as he watched Alex build with blocks. Alex, using the defense mechanism of *projection of evil,* saw Robbie's closeness as a threat rather than as a compliment to his building skills. Robbie cried out sharply when hit. The teacher turned to me and said, "Alex must just be tired." Perhaps she was not sure how to handle this deliberate and sudden hurtful action. Her response showed *denial*—she denied that there had been any aggressive intent, but she needed to tune into Alex's tendency to be suspicious of other children's motives and plan for ways to decrease his distress.

CONCLUSIONS

By addressing the ways in which we ourselves respond to stress, we gain better insights into a particular child who seems impelled to use denial or frequently accuses others of starting a fuss rather than simply admitting when he or she has done something not in accordance with classroom rules. A big help for caregivers during in-service learning sessions is to role-play effective ways to deal with scenarios such as sudden aggressive interactions.

Be aware, however, that sometimes a child's sudden aggressive actions are long-term consequences of drug exposure in the womb, rather than the consequence of family tensions, rearing styles, or personality. A first-grade teacher called and confided her terrified feelings when a child suddenly picked up a pair of scissors from her desk and tried to stab the neck of the boy sitting in front of her. That child had a history of biological assault (exposure to drugs) in the womb; her mother had taken drugs throughout the pregnancy. Teachers need a store of child development knowledge in order to decode stressful behaviors and to provide safe, nurturing environments for all children in their care.

STUDY QUESTIONS

What is stress?

Why do we need to be concerned about stressors in the lives of children and their child care providers?

How do children show us that they are stressed? Are there any telltale behavior signs?

What are some examples of short-term stressors and long-term stressors for children?

What are some consequences of prolonged stress on the body?

What are Freudian defense mechanisms, and what are some examples of these mechanisms?

SOURCES AND SIGNS OF STRESS

Interpersonal factors as well as biological personality factors often are related to stressful child behaviors. Teachers who are perceptive about differences in the *attachment security* of a child and in a child's *temperament* style will be more alert to the sources of some distressful behaviors. Caregivers who are aware of ongoing family disruptions can be more supportive while the child is in the safe, nurturing, and predictable environment of the child care facility or the school classroom. Teacher insights help them home in on more appropriate, helpful interventions for a child.

SECURE VERSUS INSECURE ATTACHMENT IN RELATION TO RESILIENCY TO CHILD STRESS

Difficult child behaviors such as having tantrums in mildly frustrating circumstances or aggression against playmates sometimes result from a child's history of insecure attachment to the parent during the first years of life. The British psychiatrist Dr. John Bowlby (1969) and

23

American psychologist Dr. Mary Ainsworth (1973) provided vivid and detailed descriptions of the differential behaviors of infants that revealed whether they were securely bonded with or insecurely attached to Mother, compared with another person. Securely attached infants preferentially smiled and vocalized to Mother. They lifted arms to be picked up when mother returned after a brief absence. They looked soberly at a stranger, but once safely in mother's arms they could then give the stranger a dazzling smile.

What is attachment? Why is it such an important aspect of early development? *Attachment* is a reciprocal and enduring emotional tie between a baby and a caregiver. Bowlby (1969) regarded this tie as biologically based and having long-term consequences for emotional well-being and disturbance. Initially in Uganda and later in Baltimore, Ainsworth (1973) meticulously described infant-toddler behaviors that were indicators of secure or insecure attachment to Mother. During lengthy home visits, she observed maternal behaviors typical with a year-old baby who seemed either securely or insecurely attached.

THE AINSWORTH STRANGE SITUATION

The Ainsworth Strange Situation (ASS) is the most well-known laboratory procedure used to document an infant's attachment status with an adult (Honig, 2002). This procedure has proved reliable and useful in many cultures and for infants who attend group care as well as for home-reared babies. During the ASS, a mom and year-old baby are in a playroom together for 3-minute episodes. The baby undergoes two separations from Mother. A strange adult is present during the first separation. No one is present with baby during the second, and therefore more stressful, separation. Ainsworth and colleagues (1971) particularly focused on the *reunion behaviors* of infants when Mom returned to the experimental playroom. Close observation revealed that at reunion, infant behaviors clustered into three major types. Ainsworth labeled the three attachment classifications to Mother as:

- *A* babies: avoidantly attached
- *B* babies: securely attached
- *C* babies: hesitantly or ambivalently attached

A babies rarely cried when Mother left; they ignored Mom at reunion. *B* babies sought and accepted maternal comfort; then they went back to explore and play with toys. *C* babies acted anxious and upset when

Mother left the room. On her return, they showed their ambivalence by seeking maternal comfort, but when picked up in the mother's arms, they squirmed to get down, and sometimes even hit out at the mother. *C* babies exhibited conflicting tendencies. They seemed to want comfort and yet seemed unable to accept comfort from Mother.

Later research explored a third insecure attachment pattern. *D* babies looked dazed and disoriented on reunion with Mom. They showed inconsistent and disorganized responses to Mother. Research showed this pattern is more likely when mothers have been insensitively intrusive or abusive (Main & Solomon, 1986).

What are the social and emotional consequences of different attachment patterns? How do they affect young children's responses to stress? Longitudinal researches indicate that the baby with secure emotional attachment to the parent has an easier time emotionally and socially years later. The securely attached baby grows up a more resilient child, sociable, confident and empathic with peers, friendly, and higher in self-esteem.

What Are the Long-Term Consequences of Insecure Attachments in Children?

What are the long-term consequences of insecure attachments that early childhood educators need to know about? Sroufe and Fleeson (1988) set out to answer this question by observing emotional and social behaviors of preschoolers for whom they had ASS assessments as 1-year-old infants. Sroufe and colleagues set up an experimental preschool. Through a one-way screen they could observe the children's interactions with peers and with the well-trained professional teachers.

As infants, some of the preschoolers had been classified as *A* babies. They had learned early on that their moms did not like close bodily contact or cuddling and were likely to act more irritable (than other moms) if a baby was needy or fussing. So the *A* infants had learned not to react much when Mom left the room during the ASS procedure, and they were likely to ignore Mom upon her return 3 minutes later. Now several years later, these *A* children acted as bullies in the classroom. The only children to whom these highly qualified teachers ever spoke sharply turned out to have been *A* babies! Teachers tended to ignore the *B* children (who had been securely attached to Mom in infancy) more than the other children. Teachers tended to be more indulgent with the *C* children. It is awesome to realize that none of the teachers of the preschoolers knew about the infancy findings of a secure or insecure classification for each child. Please note that the *D* children were too few in number to be included in this research study.

As part of this study, the researchers paired each child with a peer for a brief play session in a separate playroom. When paired with a *C* child, an *A* child behaved as a bully. The *C* child often accepted the role of victim in play; he or she might even ask the bully anxiously, "Aren't you going to tease me some more?" When a *B* child was paired in the peer play situation with an *A* child who tried to bully, then the *B* child moved away in the room to play comfortably on his own with toys. When a *C* child was paired in the separate play situation with a *B* child, then the *C* child did not behave as a victim, but that child often acted somewhat immaturely.

Thus, some stressful behaviors such as bullying in a classroom may result from insecure relationships built with a parent many years before the child entered preschool or elementary school. Teachers need to be quite alert to a child's persistent patterns of behaving like a bully or a victim in the classroom. Patience and perseverance, ingenuity, and warmth can help children treat each other in more friendly and appropriate ways. The deeper a child's trust in the loving quality and security of your caregiving, the more likely that the child will form a secure attachment with the teacher or caregiver (Honig, 2009).

THE ROLE OF TEMPERAMENT IN RESPONSES TO STRESS

Temperament is revealed not by transitory emotions (e.g., a child's shriek of delight when she catches the ball) but also by relatively enduring, consistent personality differences in feeling, thinking about, and handling life situations. Temperament plays a prominent role in how children respond to the stressors they encounter. Adult caregivers can somewhat modify inborn temperament or personality traits by their calm, insightful handling of each child. However, caregivers need to be aware of the strong role temperament plays when they observe a highly energetic, active child rushing about in the classroom or a shy child who shrinks back and refuses to participate in play.

The eight temperament traits include degree of rhythmicity in bodily functions, such as eating, sleeping, and toileting; withdrawal from or acceptance of the new; threshold for distress reaction; intensity of response to stress; eventual adaptability after experiencing stress; attention span; persistence; mood; and activity level (Thomas, Chess, & Birch, 1968). We will go over examples of each trait so that a teacher can recognize these clearly and thus be better able to figure out how to help a stressed child when temperamental traits are at play.

Clinicians cluster these traits into three main temperament types. Some labels for the three types are: 1) easygoing, 2) shy and cautious, or 3) irritable, difficult, and intensely reactive. Child psychologist Lieberman (WestEd, n.d.) narrated an excellent teaching video about temperament. She referred to the three types as "flexible, fearful, and feisty." Some children do not fit easily into one temperament category. They might show irregular sleep patterns but regular eating patterns.

GOODNESS OF FIT

No matter what the temperament type of a child, *goodness of fit* between the caregiver and the child is most important in determining how well a child adapts in the social world of the group. Caregivers are crucial players in the interpersonal world of child care. They can ensure that temperament is not destiny. More "triggery" children can grow up to become wonderful adults, kind and caring, despite their tendency toward more intense emotional responses. An aware caregiver is careful not to push a cautious child into new situations that at first provoke fearful, negative reactions. The teacher understands that this child can be lured, gradually, into comfortable enjoyment of new activities.

Goodness of fit requires that caregivers figure out their temperament styles and how they can best help each young child to adapt successfully to situations in child care regardless of temperament type. Aware of the very different ways in which temperament influences a child's response to new activities or projects, caregivers interact in ways that enliven, ease, and enrich children's lives.

USE NOTICING SKILLS FOR TUNING INTO TEMPERAMENT

Noticing skills are a powerful tool for tuning into temperament. Notice that some children have more trouble than others in accepting the new, especially an unexpected situation.

Jennie had been invited for a ride with her playmates and their daddy to go sledding at a local park. It was snowing heavily. On the way back home, the car got a flat tire. Dad left the children safely outside under a store awning. He returned to the car and got out his jack from the trunk so that he could jack up the car and replace the bad tire with a spare. His children watched with bright-eyed curiosity. But Jeannie sobbed uncontrollably, "We'll never get home. I'm scared. I'll never see my mommy again." The other children were used to their father solving small problems, such as replacing a battery on a toy that did not work, or repairing a broken toy with duct tape. They felt secure and expected that all would turn out well. They took this episode in stride and maybe even considered this mishap an adventure they could tell Mom about when they got home.

Notice that some children are very irregular in feeding, toileting, and sleep habits while others are very predictable in their daily bodily rhythms. Some children can spend a long time playing with a toy of interest. Others are highly distractible. One child keeps trying to make a mud pie with sand and water over and over, even when the pie crumbles as the child turns his pail upside down. Another child tries to fit a piece into a puzzle, but persistence is in short supply. When she does not succeed the first time, she sweeps the puzzle off the table and wanders away.

By staying alert to and aware of temperament differences, teachers are better able to fine-tune their responses to individual children. Children who are temperamentally more likely to *withdraw from the new* may avoid new playmates, refuse friendly overtures, or eye new foods suspiciously (Honig, 1997). Some children get upset even when their parents take them on interesting day trips and rides to new places. Six-year-old David found his house with its Lego drawer and computer games much more appealing than taking a car trip with his family. He refused to go with them on a short trip and shouted at his parents, "You know how to travel, sure, but you don't know how to stay!" (Ruppin, 2006, p. 4). Other children, whose parents move frequently, react differently. Craving adventures, they excitedly want to explore the new neighborhood—a chance for discoveries and making new friends.

Attuned to temperament, the perceptive teacher realizes that even mild changes, such as moving all the furniture around in the classroom during winter break, will throw some children into a tizzy. She prepares the children ahead of time and includes them in her projected plans before the holidays begin.

CONSIDER TEMPERAMENT

Directors too need to consider temperament in hiring and assigning staff. A teacher I had observed in loving interactions with young babies for many years at another center phoned and asked for help. She confided her deep dismay and fright because her current director wanted to switch her to the toddler room permanently. She reminded me, and I confirmed to her, what a gentle, loving teacher she was with babies in her care. She was not comfortable working with older toddlers. The director, when asked gently to reconsider, realized that her decision needed to reflect *goodness of fit* for the caregiver also, and she allowed the provider to continue working in the infant room.

Supervisors need to be thoughtful when arbitrarily making new teacher arrangements or asking for a sudden change in classroom assignment. During winter weeks, when more infants were absent with colds, a director decided to assign an infant teacher to the preschool room upstairs for the next several weeks. The infant teacher, very loving with the babies but reserved and shy about making a fuss, felt upset when told of this sudden change, even though it was to be temporary. She was distressed not only for herself, but for what her sudden disappearance for weeks would signify for the infants in her care.

As a teacher's aide, Ms. Addy loved her job. She enjoyed her helping role—preparing meals, washing toys, and taking little ones to the potty. The head teacher wanted to give Addy more responsibilities and thought her actions would make Addy proud of learning new skills. She asked Addy to prepare a lesson for the preschoolers on growing seeds and looking at flowers. Feeling unsure of how to develop a curricular lesson plan, and knowing very little about flowers, Addy did not respond to her head teacher. However, she called in sick for the next few days. Finally her head teacher realized that her request, rather than giving a boost to Addy, was genuinely stressing her. She went to the director and explained the situation. The director telephoned Addy and reassured her that she could continue the wonderful helpful work she had been doing in the classroom.

Children differ temperamentally not only in their threshold for experiencing stress but also in the *intensity* and *duration* of their response to distress. They differ as well in their *ability to adapt* after experiencing a stress. Some children act quite fearful and anxious if a substitute teacher comes into the classroom. They are distressed when unfamiliar grandparents come to visit the home, but they settle down fairly easily. Some children throw long tantrums if thwarted in taking another child's toy or if by chance a peer snatches a particularly loved toy they are clutching.

Not only caregivers but parents too need to gain insights into a child's temperament characteristics and how best to optimize coping techniques. While living in France and doing research in a well-baby clinic, I was able to briefly care for my grandchild, Daniel, then 18 months. As he was playing outside with a spoon and an old margarine tub in the sandbox near my apartment, a feisty toddler came running along and grabbed the spoon. Daniel, a flexible child, looked briefly at the child running away with his spoon. Turning back to the sand pile, he continued filling the pail by scooping the sand by hand. Unfazed by having his spoon taken, Daniel found a different way to keep on enjoying his play in the sandbox. The mother of the exuberant toddler who had snatched the spoon ran after her child. She called out to me that she was jealous, because her little one was a "tremblement de terre"—an earthquake!

In the restaurant, Ginny's dad, answering her demand, commented mildly that he would not be ordering dessert; she had eaten very little of the meal she ordered and instead filled up on bread although her dad had gently asked her not to. Ginny leapt out of her chair, ran over and sobbed against her dad's chest, whining and demanding dessert. She acted as if she were in despair because she was not to have a dessert, even though she had not eaten the chicken and broccoli she herself had ordered, after announcing as they all sat down to dinner that she was very hungry! Her loving parents both had noticed that Ginny usually expressed both joy and despair with far more intensity than her siblings.

When you want to consider the possibility that a particular child's stress arises from special temperament traits, ask yourself questions, such as

Do ordinary hassles from changes in curricular activities during the day appear to overwhelm this child?

Do frustration stresses seem to rise quickly and reactions suddenly reach the level of tantrum or enraged behaviors?

Does this child seem particularly sensitive to sounds, touches, tastes, or movement?

Does the child react with acute anxiety and seem to feel threatened by even mild suggestions of change or offers of new experiences, people, or foods?

Is this child in perpetual and impulsive motion in the classroom?

Is it difficult for this child to calm down once a teacher offers empathy and support?

Yes answers to the questions you pose will clarify and often confirm for you that this child's stresses may well arise from temperament challenges.

EXTERNALIZING AND INTERNALIZING STRESS

As adults we express our stress in different ways. Some of us yell a lot. Some of us get diarrhea if scared. Some adults self-medicate as a response to stress, using drugs or alcohol to decrease stress. One mother, whose older children had already been removed by social services, brought her baby for assessment and told me that taking heroin lessened her pain and anguish. Many stressed adults drug themselves with legal drugs, such as whiskey and cigarettes. In a bar, their troubles seem to vanish, and everyone around is a buddy. Some people deal with stress by compulsive behaviors, which result in serious gambling debts or compulsive sexuality that may damage spousal trust irrevocably. Some hurl accusations back at those whom they feel are attacking them. A parent accused of keeping a sloppy house with toys scattered all over yelled angrily back at the accuser that he should try taking care of little children all day!

Externalizing Children

Some externalizing youth, unable to keep up in school with peers, become truant and avoid school. Having experienced difficult childhoods, some join gangs as adolescents, practice "tough guy" behaviors, and participate in neighborhood turf battles. Their externalizing responses to stress result in aggressive and harmful actions—for themselves as well as others.

Internalizing Children

Some children are *internalizers*. Worrying a lot, they grind teeth so strongly during sleep times that they have aching jaws. Some children get severe headaches when they hear family fighting and breakdowns in civil communication. You probably have noticed how differently each child reacts to stress as you watch one child's worried frown or another child biting his lips. When parents scream and yell, some worried children have confided that they mostly run to their rooms and hide under the bed.

Watching Children's Bodily Responses for External and Internal Signs of Stress

Children's *bodily responses* are one of the telltale signs of insecurity that teachers learn to watch for. Body language shows us how much children are affected by stress. As a volunteer in a mental health association program for parents with divorce and custody troubles, I listened to parents describing how a child vomited and screamed when told the parents would be divorcing.

With a very low threshold for stress, some children respond intensely to quite mild or unintentional upsets. A little boy acts as if he has been attacked, yet a peer had *accidentally* brushed past him while galloping enthusiastically across the yard toward a desired tricycle. In the child care room another child clenched his fists, whirled around, and punched a peer as if retaliating against a perceived yet imaginary threat.

Children's tense bodies reveal the stress within. Hunched shoulders, worried frowns, twitching eyes, and head banging in the crib are telltale body signs of stress.

Lissa, a 9-year-old girl, assigned for a custody evaluation during a divorce, bit her fingernails so that they were bleeding. Her grave little face appeared more careworn than a young child's face should be. She explained, "My new stepfather doesn't know a lot about little kids, and he does have some very strict rules, but he loves my mom and I want to live with my mom." I recommended to the court that the stepfather should be required to take a parenting course. The mother phoned months later and told me that her husband was learning to be a more flexible and appropriate parent with her young children and the child's stress was somewhat relieved. Lissa's fingernail biting had ceased.

Body signs of distress can be misinterpreted. Some children show distress by acting sullen and withdrawn. A caregiver asked a classroom program consultant if perhaps a certain child (who had only been in the classroom for a few weeks) had a hearing impairment. That child totally ignored the teacher's cheerful requests to help put his blocks away in preparation for snack time. How surprised the teacher was one day to observe his prompt, helpful responses when his beloved grandpa came early to pick him up from his classroom and asked him to help put away his toys before they left. This child was particularly wary with strangers. He had not yet grown emotionally attached to his teacher. So he did indeed tune her out for a while, which puzzled and frustrated her until she understood that this was his response to the stress of a new situation.

Worried about being called on to read aloud in class, a child in first grade complains of a bad tummyache. In another case, a child who had been scolded by his second-grade teacher for giving the wrong answer to an easy arithmetic problem suddenly peed on the floor of his classroom, and his classmates ridiculed him.

Lori's teacher was very insistent on neat handwriting. Her parents brought Lori for a consultation because they were worried about her discouraged feelings regarding school. They explained that Lori felt so nervous about what the teacher ridiculed as her "itchy-skritchy" writing. I showed Lori a funny comic cartoon. She smiled at it. I gently asked her to write about it in a few sentences. She wrote something, and then looked worried, frowned, and tried to cross this out. She pressed down with the eraser so vigorously that she tore a big hole in the sheet of paper. She froze, staring at her paper with a stricken, worried look.

Classroom criticisms hurt the soul of children whose tensions come out in tight fingers and ruined homework papers.

CONCLUSIONS

Many factors, both biological and interpersonal, are related to stressful child behaviors. Teachers should be perceptive about differences in a child's behavior. In this way teachers will be more alert to the sources of some distressful behaviors. Children can internalize or externalize stress in many different ways. Your insightful observations and skillful ways of handling these stresses will support more optimal growth and development in the children with whom you work.

STUDY QUESTIONS

What is *attachment?* Why is it such an important aspect of early development?

What is *goodness of fit?* Why is goodness of fit between the caregiver and the child important?

What are *noticing skills?* Why are noticing skills an important and powerful tool?

Why is it important to take temperament into consideration when assessing stress in children?

What are some ways children externalize and internalize stress?

INSIGHTS
ABOUT STRESS

REFLECTING AND REFRAMING

Thoughtful attention to the causes and kinds of stress are one step in the ongoing process of choosing ways to defuse stressful situations for children. Teacher insights about the causes of stress will often illuminate the best way to handle child stress. Teacher *reflectivity* about hidden causes for stress or puzzling ways of showing stress is crucial in planning how to ease some stress situations for children. What are some reflections that will be helpful in choosing strategies to decrease child stress?

RECOGNIZE UNACCEPTABLE
OR WORRISOME CHILD BEHAVIORS

Recognize unacceptable or worrisome child behaviors as opportunities to think more deeply about a particular child's possible experiences with ongoing stress. You probably are well aware when a child in your group

35

habitually tattles on others or a child regularly accuses others rather than accepting responsibility for breaking classroom rules. Think about what may have happened to him. Is he punished a lot at home? Is he feeling that he does not get the attention that teachers give some of the well-behaved children in the class? Does he seem to be trying to get attention from teachers—even though he gets intense *negative* attention? Research has shown that children who are used to negative interactions with their parents at home often try to engage a teacher in the same kinds of negative interactions they are used to with adults at home (Wittmer & Honig, 1988).

REALIZE THAT DEVELOPMENTAL GROWTH MAY CAUSE STRESS

Developmental growth itself may cause stresses. A child struggles to learn a new skill, such as walking, toileting, handling an eating utensil, or talking clearly enough so that bewildered adults can understand the garbled words. What other salient developmental struggles increase stress in very young children? Learning to separate from parents and being cared for by strangers are stressful for some infants and toddlers more than for others. Developmentally expected responses of *separation anxiety* and *stranger anxiety* are quite typical. With loving attentiveness and a relaxed adult approach, these stresses ease over time as the child gains mastery of each new skill.

LEARNING TROUBLES CAN BE STRESSORS

Children unable to keep up with class requirements experience anxiety and stress. In class, a first-grade child still struggles to understand how a sound like *b* corresponds to the first letter in the word *bunny* in his picture book. His classmates, well on their way to learning to read, have already solved the *phoneme–grapheme correspondence problem* that bewilders him. Teachers need skills to provide such a child with help toward mastering the developmental task of reading.

Mild dyslexia may not be as salient and identifiable as a stress to a teacher as are behavioral disruptions. Frustrated with not being able to learn to read, Charlie chose to act out as the class clown. He went to the back of the room, turned on the sink faucet, and dunked his head until his hair was sopping wet. He then shook droplets of water all over so that all the children were laughing. One secret for alleviating the distress of a child with dyslexia is patient and skillful tutoring help in learning to read materials that focus exclusively on the child's particular personal interests.

This developmental problem provides a different kind of challenge to the teacher in comparison with helping the out-of-control, intensely active child who tries to beat up a peer he perceives as moving too close to his play project. Different stresses require different handling. Some child stresses are more likely to result from interpersonal experiences, such as being bullied in the classroom. One school-age child retained urine and felt great bodily distress. She explained to me that she was fearful of using the girl's toilet in the school because of harassment from bullying girls in the bathroom.

CHILD-DEVELOPMENT KNOWLEDGE: YOUR FIRST LINE OF DEFENSE FOR AVOIDING SOME CHILD STRESSORS

Certain child stresses arise from a child's current cognitive stage of functioning in relation to the demands and pressures put upon him or her. These stresses are eased greatly when parents and caregivers understand the different stages of sensorimotor and preoperational thinking so typical of infants and preschool children.

The caregiver placed a busy board with a lacing shoe and a slide-bolt device on the 1-year-old baby's high chair tray and asked her to try the busy board. To solve this difficult busy board, a child needs advanced sensorimotor understandings of causal mechanisms and relationships between actions as *means* and as *ends or goals.* That busy board was developmentally appropriate for a toddler but not for this infant. The baby looked puzzled as she touched some items. Then with a sweep of her hand, she threw the busy board crashing down onto the floor. The caregiver looked sad. "Don't you like any of the toys I got out for you?" she asked the baby.

Learning about different stages of cognitive development will ease caregivers' puzzlements and frustrations as well as enhance their choices of curricular materials more appropriate for each child's abilities.

Hone Mental Health *Noticing Skills*

Become a *body watcher* for child stress signs. Watch each child's signs of tension from head to toes. Does this child nervously twirl a piece of hair or suck on the ends of hair? Or pull out hair (trichotillomania)? Does she nervously bite her lips? Her fingernails? Do his eyes lack luster? Can you hardly ever coax a certain child to grin or smile, even when you have an especially interesting or joyous activity going on? Does a child have an involuntary eye twitch when he feels threatened emotionally? Does a quiet and perhaps lonely baby in the group self-stimulate by sitting on the floor and rocking his body back and forth in a repetitive pattern? Does a child cross and re-cross her legs or swing them compulsively back and forth while sitting at a desk, as she worries that the workbook material seems too difficult for her? Does a toddler refuse to nap, keep his eyes alertly open, and seem unable to relax his body? Does a preschooler masturbate compulsively during the day rather than just at naptime?

Reframe Some Child Behaviors as Developmentally Normative Rather than Naughty

Sometimes adults want little children to respond as if they were much older children with well-developed self-control skills and the ability to stop and think reasonably and rationally about their actions.

> A baby, just learning to drink from a sippy cup, kept tilting the cup too much and spilling milk on his bib or else not turning his wrist far enough and thus not getting any milk into his mouth. Watching with frustration, his caregiver murmured to him, "You're making me nervous."

Recognizing the interesting ways in which we practice a new skill until we get it just right helps the adult admire rather than feel tense about how this seesawing learning process goes onward.

Think About Current Family Pressures on a Stressed Child

Often, pressures on a child to behave more maturely than he is capable of at that time lead to frustration and aggression. Sitting on the floor, a child in my office smashed toy cars together with both hands over and over. He was 4 years old but very verbal. Thinking his verbal skills meant that he was also emotionally and socially precocious, his parents were demanding behaviors more typical of a child several years older. When reminded that he was still a little fellow, they were able to reframe his behavior as a response to stressful pressures from them. They eased up on their impossible expectations for much more emotional maturity and found themselves enjoying their son a lot more.

The more we remember developmental norms the easier will be our attempts to reframe and understand young children's behavior (Honig, 1996). Sure, Johnny may have learned to share a hunk of playdough with a peer at an art table. But learning to share is a long and complex process. If Johnny happens to have a small bag of potato chips his parent left for him, then he may loudly refuse to share a chip with another child. Prosocial behavior may come more easily in one situation, such as giving some crayons to a peer sitting at the art table. But the child may become quite distressed if forced to share his special food treat.

Rare is the toddler empathic enough to share his very own blankie with another child, but children do differ. Some toddlers do show remarkable ability to feel and respond kindly to the distress of a peer (Quan & Wien, 2006). Rheingold and Hay (1976) described the kindly behavior of a toddler about 1½ years old. When the researcher staged an accident by dropping a whole bag of toys all over the floor, the toddler exclaimed, "I help clean up dis mess!" And he did! Years later, when the researchers asked elementary school teachers to identify the most prosocial children in their classrooms, they chose the children who had been identified as the most altruistic toddlers in the earlier research.

Reflect on the Meaning of Aggressive Actions as Well as Their Causes

Reflectivity is a priceless caregiver disposition. Strong reflectivity is particularly needed when the stress in the classroom is caused by a child's aggressive action. Aggressions are stressful for teachers as well as children

(Wolfson-Steinberger, 2000). When a belligerent child lashes out in anger, promptly address both the hurt child and the aggressor in ways to nurture and calm both children, even when the causes are puzzling.

Decide Whether a Child's Outburst of Anger Is a Primary or Underlying Emotion

Decide in a given situation whether a stressed angry child is primarily angry. Is the aggression episode a clear case of conflict of interest or a response to a prior peer aggression, or is there an underlying emotion at the root of the outburst?

> Jimmy, 30 months old, has been carefully building a tower of blocks and is absorbed in play. Rosie gallops over, looks at the tall tower, then gleefully and deliberately knocks it down. Rosie has violated class rules. Jimmy's indignation is righteous. He swings out angrily at Rosie and howls for the teacher!

Sometimes a child's angry actions are a cover for an underlying emotion. An underlying emotion might be *fear* of threats of bodily harm from another child. Or a child may fear failure at a game the teacher has announced that they will play. The child has already observed that other children in the group are more skilled and competent at that game. He does not want to be teased, rejected, or ridiculed by peers. Defiant, he angrily refuses to join in the game.

Another underlying emotion might be *sadness* following a disappointment or loss. Kelly loved kittens. When she tried to draw one, her scribbles did not look at all like a kitten. Suddenly she ripped her paper to pieces and stalked off. Her anger was a secondary response to her disappointment.

Another underlying feeling might be *hunger* for adult psychological and physical attention. At group storytime, Jess jostles the other children as they are getting comfortably seated on the rug to hear the story. Seeing the commotion, the teacher often invites Jess to sit close to her while she reads. As Jess leans into teacher's body, he relaxes and is able to listen quietly. His restless fussing got him the physical nearness he so needed. A teacher may want to figure out ways to give physical hugging and lap time at other times to a needy child so that the child does not have to act out to get this coveted closeness.

Another underlying feeling might be *guilt, shame,* or *threat to a child's self-esteem.* When anger is a secondary protective or assertive emotional response, then it "both regulates and obscures the vulnerable emotional response to identity threats" (Snyder, Simpson, & Hughes, 2006, p. 235). Teachers and parents need to rethink and enlarge their conceptualization of their roles. Sure, adults must keep kids safe! Sure, we need to get kids ready to learn so that they will succeed in the intellectual tasks of schoolwork. However, an equally important role for a teacher or parent is to act as an *emotional coach.* We need to help children develop emotional intelligence and social skills as well as cognitive skills (Goleman, 2006).

Decide Whether an Aggressive Behavior Is Reactive or Proactive

Reflect on the kind of aggression you must address. Did the child have temper tantrums? Act sassy? Refuse to cooperate? Sulk or blame others? These are more likely to represent *reactive* responses. Does the child try to dominate others? Act deliberately cruel to others? Brag, boast or tease others? Pick on and bother other children? These behavior patterns are signs of *proactive* aggression (Feindler, 1995). Diagnosing aggression stress perceptively helps us clarify ways we can intervene more effectively. Making decisions about *when* to handle stresses that occur with some frequency requires reflective thinking.

Will you handle some stresses prior to or after troubles occur? Decide whether you are going to choose a *reactive intervention,* after a stress event has occurred for a child, or a *proactive intervention,* which will anticipate and prepare the children, usually in a group, for possible future stress events that may occur. "Reactive interventions include activities of cognitive understanding, emotional support, structure, control, and skill development. On the other hand, proactive interventions consist of social, cognitive, affective, and self-directed activities" that a teacher devises before a difficult situation escalates (Bloom, Cheney, & Snoddy, 1986, p. 152).

CONCLUSIONS

We cannot know all the reasons for a child's stress, but we surely need to become creative in thinking of and choosing ways to help scared, disappointed, jealous, or angry children. We need to accept philosophically that we will do our best and try a variety of techniques. Seeking supports for decreasing a child's stress, many caregivers and providers reach out and enlist family help. However, if there is a family history of abuse or neglect, Perry (1993) counseled that this sharply reduces chances for provider–parent partnership. Fortunately, positive parent and caregiver relationships are often the critical catalyst in understanding and resolving child distress (Honig, 1979).

Teachers need to reflect on and assess how well this parent–provider relationship is functioning to support each child's early development (Eliker, Noppe, Noppe, & Fortner-Wood, 1997). Some communities are fortunate to have resource and referral agencies that provide expertise. Their consultants offer to come to the center and observe classroom interactions as well as talk with teachers who have reached out for further professional help.

STUDY QUESTIONS

Why is it important to understand child development when noticing stress in children?

What are proactive and reactive behaviors?

Why should we diagnose aggression as a proactive or reactive behavior? How can we use these classifications to help children cope with stress?

What is the difference between a primary and an underlying emotion?

CHOOSING STRESS-BUSTING TECHNIQUES TO HELP CHILDREN

Ideas about causes of stress are not enough. Teachers need a cornucopia of ideas that work most of the time (or even some of the time!) to decrease stress. They will need to individualize many of the techniques they choose to ease a child's stress. However, many of the excellent resources to help adults decrease stress responses are not always applicable in working with very young children. For upset adolescents and adults, many sources of advice exist to help them deal more effectively with their own stresses (Myers & Nance, 1986); some suggestions are included in later chapters.

Many suggestions given to ease adult stress are quite helpful. But they require adult cognitive skills and abilities far above those most children can yet muster. Adults are counseled to learn yoga and meditation skills. Regular meditation by adults adds to thickness of the cortex, the region of the brain that processes ideas and sensory inputs and supports executive planning. A thicker cortex may help an adult deal better with stress. Adults are advised to keep a journal of dreams and feelings. They are advised to write down episodes of distress and how they handled them. Stress experts advise that adults need to stop thinking in terms of their present stress as a catastrophe. Adults can be guided to use cognitive skills to realize that the stress they feel now is not anywhere near as horrible as losing all one's family in an earthquake or car accident or the murderous killings in villages in Darfur, Africa. These advanced reflective techniques are not applicable with very young children.

Adults can be helped to see that *overgeneralizing* is adding to their stress. They are not worthless and the people they are so angry at in their lives are not all monsters. Adults can learn to think in shades of gray. Not all people with whom we quarrel or who say upsetting things are horrible. Some are crabby and worried; some have troubles that prey on them; some of them harbor deep resentments from their own past. But toddlers are all-or-nothing thinkers. They cannot think in shades of gray. Their responses often reflect an all-bad-or-all-good type of thinking. Daddy is the meanest because he will not let Aisha have an ice cream just before dinner. But he is the "goodest" as he rubs her back and settles her into sleep at bedtime.

Angry adults tend to overestimate the probability of negative events and underestimate their coping resources. "The antidote is learning to engage in accurate estimation" (Deffenbacher, 1995, p. 164). However, children's abilities to estimate are in short supply.

RESOURCES FOR HANDLING STRESS IN CHILDREN

Resources, including semester-long curriculum classroom packages with a focus on enhancing prosocial skills, are widely available for elementary school teachers (Honig & Wittmer, 1992). Also available are lesson plans emphasizing *skill streaming*. This is the term that Goldstein has created to describe a variety of techniques to increase prosocial skills with groups of children (McGinnis & Goldstein, 1990). Other resources (Kaiser & Rasminsky, 2003) focus more specifically with suggestions on how to decrease aggressive behaviors.

Resources for helping stressed adolescents are available from many catalogues and Internet sites. For example, videos and games dealing with gossiping, taunting, bullying, and harassment among school-age children are available at http://www.jistlife.com. The web site http://www.creativetherapystore.com offers a cognitive-behavioral program called *Stress Management for Middle and High School Youth*. One helpful board game for grade school children 8 years and older is

Solution City. Players earn Solution Squares by answering game card questions from different categories (e.g., playground, bus, school, home) and learn social problem-solving skills as they play. This stress-management board game features Angus, an anxious terrier, and Serena, a cat, as they deal with 15 common social stressors with peers, authorities, and school.

STRESS-BUSTING TECHNIQUES FOR CHILDREN

Young children cannot use adolescent or adult stress management strategies! Toddlers react to a cookie snatched away by a teasing adult as a catastrophe at that moment. They cannot use the reflective and journaling skills adults might find helpful. Engaging in accurate estimations is difficult for young children. An example is the shepherd child Amahl (in the opera *Amahl and the Night Visitors*) who has just viewed the star of Bethlehem. He comes into their hut excitedly to tell his mother that he has seen a star with a tail as long as the sky. Enthusiastic exaggeration is often typical of young children's thinking.

Adults need techniques and skills that are attuned to a *wide* variety of younger children's stresses in relation to their emotional and cognitive abilities. They need compassionate understanding of children's fears (Hyson, 1979). Adults need perceptive thinking skills and courage in decision making to choose activities and interactions to alleviate stresses in younger children. Teachers can choose stress-busting techniques from many domains. Crucially, teachers need to *initiate* a more loving interpersonal relationship with a particular child. Sometimes changes arise from group talks with the children. Some resolutions of stressful incidents arise from discussions in partnership with parents. Some techniques involve changes in the environment.

Change a Child's Environment

How we choose our responses depends on the type of stress we note. Some child stresses occur because a particular care setting may not be the most harmonious environmental match for a child. A toddler was biting aggressively and frequently in a large center despite all the concerned ways in which teachers tried to help. They had shadowed him, given frequent positive attention, and pinned a mouthing toy safely to his jacket so that he could bite down hard on that toy when he felt the need to bite. They reminded him to use his biter when he felt the need to bite.

Sometimes he remembered. Most times he could not. Eventually, a move to a small, family child care worked better to decrease biting behaviors. Large-group care was not the best environmental fit for this toddler.

Be Patient

Adjustment to group care may take more time for some children. Some children need very gradual introductions to child care. They need a parent close by for some hours for many days before they will venture to explore the child care room. Others venture easily into the classroom, exploring toys with zest. A child whose native language is not English may take longer to adjust to group care. If such a child's distress seems to be ongoing, try to find a volunteer speaking the child's native language to come in and cuddle and talk with an infant or child whose distress has been lasting for weeks. Often the discomfort of child care wears off fairly quickly with that extra soothing ingredient of hearing talk in the familiar tongue of the family.

Expect Adjustment to Vary Over Time

Not all children become more smoothly adjusted to the group as time goes on. Some children act quite well adjusted to child care and then after a few months suddenly feel insecure. They may be growing into a more mature cognitive awareness of separation. Offer lots of body-nurturing care when the child shows an uneven progress in adapting to group care.

Lou, 16 months old, had seemed quite happy in child care with his teacher, Mr. Avrom. Suddenly one day, a few months later, Lou acted very demanding and crabby. He wanted to be held in arms a lot. His upset behavior was puzzling. It was as if he suddenly realized that his mama was not there. They were separated. When would he be with her again? Mr. Avrom, lovingly attuned to this probable reason, held Lou in arms and cuddled him a lot during that day. A few days later, Lou settled back into comfort in the classroom. Unfortunately, the supervisor, noticing the toddler cuddled in his caregiver's arms, reprimanded the teacher, saying, "Put him down. He knows how to walk. This is a school." The teacher gently tried to explain the toddler's need for more holding for that short time.

Supervisors as well as parents and teachers need to learn the secrets of understanding and nurturing children's emotional and social development and finding ways to alleviate the initial stress of the newness and strangeness of the child care world.

Provide Wraparound Care

Changes in conceptualizing class organization may alleviate stresses for infants. The fewer the number of caregivers a child has during the early years, the easier it is for very young children to feel secure. *Wraparound care* refers to a process in which the same loving, long-term teachers provide care during a baby's first 3 years. Wraparound care can decrease stress and increase emotional well-being for babies and toddlers (Essa, Favre, Thweatt, & Waugh, 1999; Howes, 1999).

Be Sensitive to Possible Sensory Integration and Processing Deficits

Even the most loving interpersonal approaches may only work when a teacher is attuned to a child's possible sensory integration or processing deficits. For example, some children are not comfortable with touch. Touch that is too light or gentle feels extremely uncomfortable to children with sensory difficulties. They require more vigorous pats to feel comfortable. Some children's skin feels extremely irritated just by the inside tags of a tee shirt.

Some children have trouble processing information when there is too much noise. They shut out the world by closing their eyes. They act defiant with teachers if forced to go to the gym or outdoor playground. Running-around time with the other children causes panic, not joy. Unable to tolerate the stress of loud commotion, one child even created a fantasy that scary monsters were besieging him. He squeezed his eyes shut and was not even able to listen to teachers trying to talk with him when he got upset. He put his hands over his ears if too many kids were yelling and screaming joyously at gym time, and he often refused to go to gym.

One student with sensory processing troubles confided that she acted "dumb" in her schoolwork in the classroom. She figured that if she did this, then at outdoor recess time none of the other children would choose her for the physically arousing running games in which she did not want to participate. Unfortunately, her way to cope was to get poor grades so the other children would think she was not a good choice for their rough-and-tumble games on the school playground.

Greenspan (2006), a psychiatrist who works with children who are sensory reactive, suggested

> At the beginning of the year, consider how each child in your classroom reacts to each of the senses' pathways. . . . Some children find high-frequency sounds, like opera singing, very aversive. Others find low-frequency sounds, like the vacuum or the boiler, very difficult to tolerate. . . . Some find bright light, even sunlight, very harsh and do better with subdued lighting. . . . Some children are finicky eaters because they are very sensitive to the smell or the texture of food. (pp. 22–23)

Greenspan also explained that some children are so *underreactive* rather than *overreactive* that they deliberately seek out more sensation. They want to bang into everything or create loud noises. Some underreactive children run around all the time to create movement.

How can we accommodate the distresses of children with sensory integration or processing difficulties? When the sensory difficulty is with touch, make sure the child wears only soft cotton clothing. Provide soft cushions at circle reading time. Remember to pat a child's back firmly if that child is stressed by soft or tentative touch. Pick up a baby intolerant of soft touch and hold that baby on your shoulder with your cheek firmly pressing baby's cheek as he looks out over your shoulder.

Define Terms for Children Whose Verbal Interactions Distress Their Peers

Not all aggressions are physical. Some children are more adept at psychological harassment. They call a peer a bad name. Children tattle on a peer as a way to get that child chastised by an adult. Sometimes children tattle to look good in the teacher's eyes. Teachers need to explain to children the difference between *tattling* to get a playmate into trouble, and *telling* the responsible adult something in order to keep children safe in the classroom. Some teachers have a "tattle bear" in the classroom. When children feel like tattling because they are exasperated at someone taking too long with the tricycle they want to ride, or they are in another socially stressful situation where no child is actually harmed, then the upset children can go and tell "tattle bear" the trouble. Children need a teacher's clarification of when a trouble requires a teacher's help. Explain how important it is to come tell the adult about a child's skinned knee, about a friend so frightened that he refuses to try to climb down from the climbing bars, or a peer with a nosebleed.

Provide a clear message that just because a classmate will not give up a turn he has just started with a toy, it is not okay to denounce the peer for not sharing. This is a trouble that a child can whisper to "tattle bear" rather than announce to the teacher.

Define Bullying Clearly So that Children Will Report It

Bullies are a particular distress for peers in school situations. For school-age children, "assertive, funny, and unexpected responses are the best comebacks against bullying" (Orpinas & Horne, 2006, p. 239). The following information lists some suggestions for school-age children who are faced with a bully. Also listed are sample dialogues that describe a potential interaction between a bully and a victim. The last sample dialogue also lists a potential interaction between a bully and a bystander.

Make fun of the tease, not the bully.

Bully: Look at your shoes. Did you get them in the dump?

Victim: You mean this isn't the latest style?

Accept or agree and move on.

Bully: Are you afraid to fight?

Victim: Yes I am. Do you have any other questions?

Reframe to a positive.

Bully: Hi, Shorty!

Victim: Well, as my mamma used to say, good things come in small packages.

Be assertive.

Bully: [Pinches a female classmate on the buttocks]

Victim: Stop it. That is wrong! Pinching is sexual harassment. It is against school policy, and I have to tell the teacher.

Bully: What are you, a tattletale?

Victim: I think that you need to learn the difference between tattling and reporting.

Talk about the behavior.

Bully: [Pushes the student from behind while he is standing in the cafeteria lunch line]

Bystander: You must be new at this school. We don't push kids around in our school. Pushing is against the school rules. (Orpinas & Horne, 2006, pp. 240–241)

These are useful suggestions for school-age children. However, for the toddler with little language, or the preschooler who is fearful and terrified when bullied, teachers need a wider repertoire to cope with a variety of bullying behaviors. Firmly and clearly refuse to accept bullying behaviors. Be sure to help children realize that they must indeed come to the teacher if another child does or says something that makes them feel scared or hurt.

Bullying in older preschoolers may take subtle forms. "Gender play preferences of females and their play interaction scenarios are perceived as a *danger* to be avoided by boys who want to be accepted into the world of male peer play" (Honig, 2006, p. 384). Teachers need to find creative ways to nurture cross-gender play so that boys are not stigmatized for enjoying family-type play scenarios. One suggestion is to rename the dollhouse the *house corner* so that boys feel more comfortable to playact in family scenarios.

In a nationwide study of bullying in high schools, troubling findings indicated how widespread this stress is and what an agony it entails for so many students (Garbarino & DeLara, 2002). These researchers soberly advised that when bullying is a problem in the classroom, this stress needs to be handled by using as many strategies as possible, including individual interaction with the bully and the victim, vigorous group work in the classroom, and enlisting the support of parents when possible.

In the book *Nobody Knew What to Do: A Story About Bullying* (McCain, 2001) one boy finally realized that all the other kids were very scared of the bullies on the playground. At recess time the bullies were beating on Ray, a quiet child. The other children were afraid to come to help Ray lest they too get beat up. So then the boy hero in this story bravely decided to go and tell his teacher all about the situation. When she heard about the bullying, the teacher then went to the school principal. Together the adults walked out on the playground to ensure that no more bullying occurred. The teacher and principal also phoned the parents for a group meeting to talk about how to abolish bullying.

Help Children Handle Jealousy

Jealousy is a stress for some preschoolers when a second child has been born and is getting lots of attention at home. Fortunately for teachers, older preschoolers have more cognitive capabilities. They are beginning to be able to hold two different and sometimes opposite ideas together. A blue circle can be sorted into a pile for blue items. It can be sorted into a pile for circles. It has both characteristics. So too can the challenge of jealousy be experienced as two different feelings.

An older sibling in preschool can be really glad that he or she will be able to teach the new baby sibling lots of things. The new baby lights up as soon as the older sibling comes into sight. The baby giggles more when the older sibling plays Pat-a-cake or other games. But the preschooler does indeed resent all the time and attention Momma and Papa give this little one. The preschooler has to balance different feelings. By the preschool years, the *absolute* toddler mind, with things perceived as either wonderful or terrible, has modulated with development. A talk with preschoolers about double feelings that have both happy and grumpy aspects is a positive action to help children who are wrestling with such dual feelings.

Try describing the following scenario: A child goes to a birthday party and loves the birthday cake, ice cream, and fun games. But that child also feels jealous that the birthday child received a handheld video game system as a gift just like the one that the child himself has been longing to have! Feelings of gladness are mixed with jealous feelings.

When you introduce the idea of having different feelings at the same time, then a preschooler struggling with jealousy problems may be able to handle confused feelings better. In the case of the preschooler who is faced with a new baby sibling, this older sibling may feel not only jealousy but also a not-so-secret pride at his or her ability to captivate the new baby into giggles and smiles. Realizing these dual feelings, the preschooler may find it easier to calm down. New insights give the older sibling confidence that he or she is really going to be a winner in the long run when dealing with conflicting feelings about the new baby.

CONCLUSIONS

Teachers can use a variety of stress-busting techniques to decrease stress in children. Teachers may need to individualize many of the techniques listed in this chapter. Strategies for handling a child's stress, such as the ones suggested in this chapter, may provide a helpful beginning for classroom teachers and professionals who will be creating their own personal collection of strategies that have worked in decreasing stress in the children they are nurturing.

STUDY QUESTIONS

What are some stress-busting techniques for children?

What are some suggested ways to advise a child to handle a bully at school?

Why is it important to explain the difference between *telling* and *tattling* to children?

How can you help children handle jealousy?

CHAPTER 5

PERSONALIZING STRESS-REDUCING STRATEGIES FOR CHILDREN

Every teacher needs a personal supply of strategies that work most of the time to calm children and increase classroom peacefulness. These techniques allow the adult to personalize and enhance positive interactions with each individual child. Included in this chapter are some stress-reducing strategies for children. No one stress technique works every time in every situation with every child. As you become a seasoned child observer, your special knowledge of each child will help you adapt techniques to a particular child in a particular situation. For example, you may find that picking up a child and holding him close in a big hug is a good method for calming that child during a challenging interaction. Your ingenuity and perceptive insights will help you to adapt methods to decrease the child's stress.

PROVIDE SOOTHING PHYSICAL CONTACT AND VERBAL REASSURANCE

Touch is magic; touch is crucial (Honig, 2002). Use soothing touch whenever possible to calm an upset child. Caress a child's back with long, soothing strokes using an outstretched palm. When a tiny child is suffering from separation anxiety during the early times after entering care, holding and stroking the child are especially important to decrease stress. An infant carrier such as a kangaroo pouch works well for soothing a tiny baby with your body warmth and the rhythms of your movements. In the days after enrollment, a toddler often needs more cuddling time when suffering stranger anxiety or separation distress. Yet this same toddler can grin and run boldly away from a caregiver in a delighted show of his autonomy when he is feeling comfortable in the child care situation.

Give a Calming Massage

If a child is perpetually getting into disagreements with other children, set aside a few minutes twice a day as your special time with that child. Use this time to massage that child's back and shoulders, arms, and fingers with lotion; this strategy seems to work like magic for many children. Some preschoolers will even request a soothing rub with "magic" lotion when they are feeling distressed.

Watch an infant massage video. Learn specific gentle strokes, such as Indian milking, Swedish milking, paddlewheel, sun and moon, and other strokes that relax babies' bodies. Massage calms the soul and the body. Babies who are massaged regularly or daily begin to respond to massages with smiles and relaxation (Leboyer, 1976). Locate lotion with colorful sparkles inside. Some preschoolers who need daily arm and hand massages to bring down tense feelings are sure that lovely lotion with sparkling colors has even more magic to soothe worries.

A child who has been abused may stiffen and flinch if you approach frontally to caress the child. Try back rubs and soothing pats on the shoulder in your initial attempts to increase loving touches for that child.

Use Lowered Voice Tones

Use lowered voice tones when trying to calm an upset child. Speak slower and with a soothing, even hypnotic, reassuring tone. The calmness in your voice brings down stressful feelings. Lower rather than raised tones in response to the child's tense exhibition of distress will soothe the child's psyche. This technique often works well also with an adult who is frazzled, sharp toned, and sounds upset on the phone or at a parent conference.

Use a Child's Name Frequently and Lovingly

You have noticed how proud preschoolers are when they learn how to write some letters of their name. Now they can "sign" their own pictures to bring home for parents to display on the refrigerator. Some 3-year-olds not only can make those letters but can sound them out when coached by a parent. Use each child's name often with loving intonations.

When babies are only a few weeks old, they love to listen for their name. Held in arms, a baby turns her head to find and focus on the face of the person softly calling her name. If a baby wakes up cranky from a nap, softly sing a waking-up song that you create on the spur of the moment. Mention baby's name a lot during the song. He will quiet himself in order to hear his own name; when he has self-soothed, you will more easily be able to pick him up for a cuddle, a diaper change, and a satisfying feeding (Honig, 2005). Incorporate each child's name in the group into a greeting song in the morning. Use any sing song melody with which you are familiar such as the following: "Good morning little yellow bird, yellow bird, yellow bird. Good morning little yellow bird who are you?" Each child answers, singing out his or her name ("My name is . . . ," sung in a sing-song voice), as you go around smiling in turn into the eyes of each of the seated children participating in this morning greeting song.

TAKE THE
CHILD'S PERSPECTIVE
AND PROVIDE OPPORTUNITIES
AND SPACES FOR SELF-SOOTHING

Children with high self-esteem are less likely to be overwhelmed by perceived threats or stresses in their lives. When you genuinely show your pleasure in the *child's* sources of interest and pleasure, the child feels validated as a person. It is helpful to tune into a child's wondering curiosity to enhance a child's self-esteem. The resulting self-assurance is a protective factor to ameliorate the effects of stress. This adult respect is especially important for a child who has caused more than a fair share of upsets in the group. Kaiser and Rasminsky (2003) provide a lovely example.

> Sixteen 4-year-olds were running to the oak tree at the far end of the field with one teacher at the front and the other at the rear. Everyone but Michael, that is. He ran off to the right. Instead of yelling at him to join the others, the second teacher followed him. When she reached him, he was smelling some small purple flowers. The snow had finally melted, and spring was just beginning. He had caught a glimpse of purple and wanted to investigate.
>
> The teacher called the other children to see what Michael had found. Everyone started to talk about the flowers, their color, and spring. They decided to continue their outing looking for signs of spring. The other children asked for Michael's help, and he had a great time playing outside. Had the teacher insisted he join the others without showing any interest in his find, his self-esteem would have been bruised, and he would have been frustrated. To get the acknowledgment he needed, he probably would have behaved inappropriately. Instead, seeing things from his perspective turned events around. Not only had this become a wonderful spontaneous science lesson, but the other children all thought that Michael was pretty smart, and he ended up feeling very proud of himself. (p. 108)

Provide Unobtrusive Help When a Task Is a Bit Too Difficult for a Child

Children can accomplish some tasks on their own after trying hard. Others are too easy or too difficult. Children get restless and bored when toys or tasks are too easy. They feel frustrated when tasks are too challenging. The Russian child-development theorist Vygotsky (1978) taught that teachers are priceless in supporting child learning and accomplishment when a task is just a bit too difficult at the child's present level of development. Then a teaching adult provides just that bit of help that will result in further child learning and satisfaction. Vygotsky used the term the zone of proximal development (or ZPD) for the difference between what a child can do on his or her own compared with what the child can do with adult help. With the assistance of an adult, a child will be able to succeed at a cognitive or social learning task beyond what he or she could have accomplished alone (Daniels, 2005; Langford, 2005).

Tamar sat on Mr. Jonathan's lap. She was trying to build a tower of small nesting blocks but was having trouble getting them to stay put so that she could add another block on top. Mr. Jonathan steadied her elbow unobtrusively with his hand. Tamar relaxed and smiled happily as she was then able to arrange the stacking block so it fit just right on top of the lower block.

Decide how much help is needed and how to provide that help in such a way that the child succeeds without the adult doing the task.

Accept a Child's Self-Comforting Needs

Have you noticed how beautifully some young children find ways to self-comfort when stressed? They pop a thumb into their mouth. They rub their treasured blanket on a cheek. In a pew at a religious service, a mom kept gently shushing her vocalizing 15-month-old, who was sitting on her lap. The little girl looked down, rummaging in the sack her mom was carrying, and drew her pacifier out of its plastic case. Triumphantly and happily she popped the pacifier into her mouth, while her whole facial expression brightened cheerfully. She solved the problem her own way!

Be generous in allowing "lovies" (special blankets or plush animals) at naptime. Some children have a really difficult time with separation from parents when they attend child care. Even when children adjust fairly easily, when they are tired or perhaps coming down with an illness they feel more stressed and need the comfort of their lovey. Make sure that each child has a safe place in a cubby for the special lovey that helps the child relax when out of sorts or upset.

If you feel uncomfortable with using lovies for preschoolers, try to focus on the child's needs for now, rather than on worries that a child will be carrying his special blanket off to college years later! Surely we do not expect an adult, nervously preparing for an important business presentation, to take along a blanket for comfort. Research shows that caregivers are indeed sensitive and aware of infant and toddler needs for their pacifier or lovey for comfort when distressed (Honig, Kim, Ray, & Yang, 2006). But often a preschool-age child still needs his or her comfort object to feel calmed. Keep each child's special comfort object in a cubby for use at nap times. Just as many children suck thumbs well into the preschool years when they feel nervous or anxious, many children need their special lovey, whether it is a soft animal or small blanket, to cuddle with at naptime. Group care often means learning to share. But a lovey is a special tension-reducer that each child has cognitively created with awesome creativity for his own special self-soothing. Reassure the children that at naptime each can indeed settle into rest with a lovey if they wish.

Sometimes a piece of a loved teacher's clothing can calm a distressed child who is prone to sudden aggressive actions. In a center, while the teacher was reading a story to a small group of preschoolers, Sandy suddenly bent down and bit his neighbor hard on the arm. The teachers had talked about what they might do. But Sandy's sudden, impulsive hurtful actions continued and became very frustrating and scary for the children. Sandy's mom shrugged off the teachers' concerns and said that her boy was a real "he-man." The solution to this classroom stress was found in the relationship Sandy had developed with Mr. Lars, one of the teachers. Sandy, whose daddy had abandoned the family before his birth, was deeply attached to Mr. Lars. Sandy seemed able to master impulses to hurt others and remain quietly attentive when Mr. Lars worked with him one-to-one on a puzzle or took him on his lap and read him a story. Mr. Lars had noticed that Sandy adored his ties. What worked to help Sandy gain inner control was his deep longing to wear his beloved teacher's tie. Sandy learned that Mr. Lars would let him have the privilege of wearing one of his ties as long as Sandy refrained from hurting another child. If Sandy did lose self-control, then the tie was taken away and put up on a shelf for the rest of that day. Finding *personalized* techniques to decrease stress and to increase a child's self-control is a creative challenge for care providers (Honig, 2008).

Some children fixate on one toy or activity to comfort their inner upset feelings. This may remind us of the way the comic strip character Linus rubs his blanket against his cheek as he sucks his thumb for dear life in order to reach a dreamy, peaceful state until, alas, Lucy or Snoopy the dog comes along to snatch his blanket away!

In the Children's Center, 5-year-old Robbie, upset by his parents' screaming fights at home, used to lie on the floor and turn the pages of Sendak's (2003) book *Where the Wild Things Are.* He was able to calm his inner feelings of helplessness in his real life by turning the pages over and over. The wild monsters pictured in the book are safely contained within those pages. In *Where the Wild Things Are,* Max is a little boy who has defied his mom. Sent to his room, he uses his imagination to sail off to an island where a crowd of monsters dances in frenzy. Later in the story, Max feels strong enough to decide to leave the monsters behind and sail home. Back in his bedroom, Max finds that his mama has left his supper on a night table right by his bed. Choosing this book over and over, Robbie gained reassurance to face his own inner monsters without fear that he would be swept away by their angers and frenzied antics. His compulsive need to look at this book was his way of addressing his stress. He chose this technique on his own, and his perceptive teachers noticed this and respected his strong need and his solution.

Brief Bouts of Compulsive Behavior May Temporarily Soothe a Stressed Child

Freddy, a preschooler, stressed by tensions at home, chose to calm himself by pushing a miniature car through the first floor of a toy playhouse set on a low table in the classroom. He watched carefully as he pushed the car through the back door. The car crashed through the back door of the cardboard house onto the floor. Then he would pick up the toy car and send it hurtling through the house and crashing down. Over and over, he reenacted the crashing experience that paralleled the experiences he was having at home. His insightful teacher realized that this repetitive behavior seemed to calm his tensions. Should she have tried to distract him? Should she have tried to lure him into a less solitary and compulsive activity, or should she wait a while? Choosing *ways to handle* and *when to handle* child stresses surely challenges our professional decision-making and expertise. In this case, the teacher wisely decided to let Freddy continue. The repetitive play seemed to calm him as he concentrated on the game for about 5 minutes. Then she was able to call the children, including Freddy, together for story time.

Primary school teachers comment that sometimes a child fixates on a hand-held video game, such as a Game Boy, and seems to tune out what else is going on. Children sometimes hunch over that type of toy as if they are thus able to shut out the world of badgering adults. They act as if their inner well-being depends on the electronic device. They cling to that toy, and the compulsive need for this electronic comfort object may reveal underlying life stresses, although a teacher may not know what those stresses are.

Wise adults recognize the variety of ways in which child behaviors and interactions reveal their inner distress. Sometimes a comfort object is symbolic, such as blocks a child arranges a certain way to represent a special comfort object. Paley (1990) vividly describes 4-year-old Jason's use of this technique to decrease his stress. Month after month in her classroom, he arranged blocks as a helicopter. Then he determinedly played at being a helicopter. His fixation on this role allowed him to zoom away over inner troubles and ambivalences. His private fantasy play about this precious possession helped him cope with ambivalent feelings about separation and danger. Paley realized that Jason felt lost at school away from home. She thought deeply about his determined need to pretend to be, to repair, to find seats for, and to fly his imagined helicopter. Insightfully, his teacher reasoned that this "will be his agent of rescue, from school to home. The ultimate fear and loss, Jason's [play] tells us, is separation" (p. 147).

Create a Cozy Retreat

A stressed child needs to know there is a safe, quiet space in the class-room to unwind. Some teachers, already sensitive to this need, have placed a beanbag chair with cozy pillows in a quiet corner. They arrange picture books invitingly on a low shelf nearby. Some teachers set a soft mattress or a blanket in a quiet corner on the floor with pillows. One teacher set up a canopy corner for children to unwind. She enlisted parents to help set up sturdy, safe poles well anchored on the floor near a back wall of the room. Over the pole tops they draped a gauze curtain. They placed a light washable rug and some pillows on the floor below, to signal a safe space where a youngster could go and rest when upset. Enchanted with this new cozy space, the preschoolers suggested placing small glittery sticker stars over the gauze. They all helped press the sticky stars on the gauze. After the canopy was in place, when the children were lying down to relax, they looked up happily at their "starry sky," the gauze canopy overhead.

Store a Personal Photo Book in Each Child's Cubby

Enlist family support to provide pictures of each family member. Ask for photos where the child is in a loving pose with a family member. If the family cannot provide photos, try to find community volunteers who can come to the center and, with the family's permission, take photos of each child with a family member at a special center event, such as a potluck supper. When possible, add photos from special family trips to the zoo or to a family reunion. If a child is wandering aimlessly in the classroom, ask the child to go get the special picture book. Sit snuggled with that child. Slowly turn the pages with him. Seeing loved ones in photos cheers a child. If the child is verbal, ask about each picture and let your genuine pleasure at this sharing relax the child as you sit cozily reminiscing together.

HOW TO PREVENT CHILD STRESSORS
Reduce Clutter

If a child is overwhelmed visually by too many stimuli and is unable to concentrate on one activity without switching attention constantly, rethink your space decorations. Scan classroom spaces to reduce the stress of too much stimulation for the child who cannot cope. Colorful child paintings hung on every wall of your gaily-decorated room may feel cheery for most of the children. For the oversensitive child, however, the bright colors clustered on every wall may feel overwhelming.

For the child who is *underreactive*, provide what Greenspan called "modulation and regulation games." Play games where you move with the child from very slow to fast to very fast. Try this game going in the other direction, from extremely fast to very slow. Have a preschooler bang on a drum. Urge him to watch as well as feel the differences in speed used. Ask the child in a one-to-one activity to produce soft voice sounds and then louder sounds and then go from louder to softer. These activities permit the child to control levels of sensory stimulation and become aware of how his own body produces these sensations.

Find Alternative Spaces for a Child Stressed by Group Play Time in a Gym

Think creatively when a child storms about and refuses to go to gym time with the group. Teachers in one school told me how bewildered and frustrated they felt with one child. He stubbornly lashed and kicked out at them when they announced that it was time for gym play. Remember that sensory-processing troubles may be the cause of the commotion. Brainstorm together how to find an alternate safe space for that child. Could the director set up a special place in the office for the child to play quietly on his own, rather than allowing him to fall apart in anguish because he cannot yet tolerate the noise and galumphing about that most children enjoy during gym time or outdoor play? Child stress may well decrease when adults tune into a child's sensory integration difficulties and find a practical solution. Teachers need to become astute detectives to figure that particular stress behaviors signal sensory sensitivities. Each child requires an individualized helpful approach.

Accept Some Messiness as Children Work

Kids can be messy. Thank goodness for soap and water. Thank goodness for smocks and plastic cover-ups. Children will be more likely to take a chance on new experiences, such as finger painting, if they know that you accept some messiness and will help them clean up in a matter-of-fact and calm manner while appreciating their new adventurousness. When adults are too strict, some young children will not venture to try any messy activity, such as clay or cornstarch goop, even when they do not have sensory integration difficulties.

> Cobie did not want to use playdough or finger paint, or mess with shaving-cream art. He was comfortable painting with a brush at the easel. But he was distressed if his fingers felt sticky or messy. Aware of his lack of comfort with sticky stuff, his teacher did not force Cobie to use the same materials as the other children when very goopy, hands-on art activities were scheduled.

Tell Children Exactly What Will Happen Ahead of Time

Mild cognitive processing difficulties may be the reason a child balks at a teacher suggestion. Tessa became very tense when a field trip was announced. Knowing that Tessa needed to know *exactly* what was going to happen, when it would happen, and how they would be going, the teacher took time to explain patiently in easy-to-understand phrases. Her teacher spoke in short, calm phrases about the planned class trip to the flower garden and the playground in a nearby park. She lured Tessa into anticipation of sniffing the delicious smell of a pink hyacinth flower in the park. Understanding the unique emotional make-up of each child furthers our ability to decrease stress and increase feelings of comfort and ease in their lives.

Use Your Reframing Skills to Understand a Child's Misbehavior Better

If a new child in the school is acting bossy with the others who are shunning him, remind yourself that easing into a group of children already quite comfortable and familiar with one another can be hard for kids. Bossiness turns off peers. You need to help the newcomer find another way to feel okay in the group. But as the teacher or caregiver, you understand the reasons for the new child's acting this way.

There is another child who is crabby and acting out of sorts. He could be acting this way because his mom is in the hospital having a new baby. Even though Grandma is taking good care of him at home, he feels anxious. When a child seems to be messing about, sometimes you will feel more at ease if you reframe this behavior as scientific exploration.

When a baby takes a piece of bread; squeezes it in his fingers; dips it in the milk remaining in his cup on the high chair tray; pulls up the soggy, drippy mass; squishes it in his fingers; and looks at it in wonder before he tries tasting it, this baby is not trying to make more work for the caregiver. He is a budding scientist who has just experimented with transformations of matter! He has learned that the piece of bread sure looks different when dipped in milk. He has learned that a solid piece of bread does taste different from a wet drippy one. You can even smile as you wisely conclude that your little scientist has learned something about transformation of matter as you observe this interesting bit of misbehavior, now reframed as budding scientific exploration (Honig, 1996).

REDIRECT RATHER THAN REPRIMAND
Create a Diversion

Sometimes with tiny children, lengthy explanations are wearying for the adult and for the toddler. A toddler reacts with intense upset if she cannot have a specific toy that another child is still using. The *distraction technique* often defuses such a stressful situation, even though we may be tempted to launch into a long discussion about an inappropriate toddler behavior. If the misbehavior was not serious, move a child more quickly out of stress mode by using the distraction technique.

A toddler holding a toy is intent on chasing after a peer. He looks as if he intends to bop the boy with that toy. Instead of a long lecture, you may choose to pick up the child in your arms lovingly. Twirl him around to face toward where other toddlers are animatedly pounding a pegboard, playing with train tracks, or climbing a geodesic dome with a teacher's help. Start to walk toward the highly interesting activity. While walking, talk happily about that wonderful activity.

This technique is also called the *magic triangle* technique (Honig, 1982a). The new interesting event can be conceptualized as the apex of a personal triangle, rather than just a focus on the interacting adult and the child, conceptualized as the two base points of the magic triangle. Get a child fascinated and absorbed in a topic, event, activity, view, or storybook so that activity becomes more interesting for the child than fussing or acting negatively. Have you noticed that as you engage the child's curiosity and interest, she or he wants to attend to the interesting event even more than to act cranky or upset?

During a rainy day, the children were grumpy because the weather did not permit outdoor playtime. The teacher carried a cranky toddler in her arms to a window and then pointed out what was going on outside. Together they watched as raindrops slithered down the windowpane. They noticed one passerby struggled with an umbrella, and the wind blew his umbrella inside out. The teacher talked about how bad that man must be feeling. She wondered aloud about what might happen. Outside the man was getting soaking wet. The teacher pointed out that his umbrella was wrecked. The toddler soon became absorbed in this event, and his mood changed from cranky to alert and interested.

Try Gentle "Magic"

Young children with an intense temperament may react with fright or anguish if they fall down and get a scrape that bleeds. Others accept some bumps or bruises, pick themselves up, and go on playing. Your "magic" can soothe stress in some situations! Have you noticed that if a toddler comes to you with a boo-boo and asks you to kiss it, as soon as you murmur nurturing words and kiss that scratch or bump, the child is then often able to run back to play? Sometimes simple "magic," such as your "magic" kiss, works wonders!

> To ease children's stress, a teacher hung up a "magic" feather duster near the front door on a classroom wall. In a classroom where a seasoned teacher used this technique, a child entered one morning feeling mad and frustrated from all of the rush and yelling at home. The preschooler told her teacher as soon as she entered the classroom, "You better get down the magic feather duster, Ms. Carol, and take away all the bad vibes!" (Honig, 2004b).

Get the children used to the idea that when they feel tense and aggravated as they come into class you will be glad to use the "magic" feather duster carefully and gently. Brush their clothes, from the shoulders downward, to clear away tensions.

THE ART OF QUESTIONING AND SUPPORTING SELF-ESTEEM

Use Socratic Open-Ended Questions to Engage Children's Interest

Most of the questions teachers pose require a *yes* or *no* answer or have one correct answer ("Do you need to go potty? What color is the doggie?"). These are called convergent questions. When you use *Socratic*, or open-ended, questions, (sometimes called divergent questions) you are more likely to intrigue and challenge a child. Research by Sigel and Saunders (1979) revealed that divergent questions help a child *distance* from an actual event in the present. The child is motivated by your questions to recall and describe a past event or think about a future happening. Open-ended questions stimulate a child to communicate more, and they enhance intimacy between child and adult. "What did you have to eat for your picnic yesterday? What can you do to comfort Jimmy who is crying? What are some favorite games you like to play with your cousin when she comes over? Which are your special Yu-Gi-Oh cards? Tell me about why these are such special cards. Thanks for teaching me about the cards."

Children enjoy explaining to adults about a topic dear to their interests, such as their pet iguana or their Pokemon cards. Children who are acting inappropriately may become all absorbed in explaining their ideas and interests to a genuinely interested adult, especially when they feel they know more about a topic than the teacher does! Your genuine interest as you continue asking Socratic questions boosts their self-esteem.

Use Socratic Questions to Find Out More About a Particular Child's Fears

Preschoolers have many fears—of witches, of robbers, of bogeymen, or of bad monsters whom they have watched on scary television programs. Levine (2004) reminded us that we must respect children's terrified fears, so real to them, and yet find ways to reassure them. She explained how important it is to have a dialogue with the child.

> Noah was a 4-year-old who had been enrolled in my preschool for a few months. . . . I was shocked when I entered the classroom one morning and he ran from me screaming, "Stay away from me!" His terror was so intense. The problem, it seems, were my new shoes. They were black, and according to Noah, witches wear black shoes. [The teacher left the classroom, took off her shoes, and was able to return just wearing socks. She sat down with Noah and asked gentle questions.] He made it clear I was only a scary witch if I was wearing the black shoes. Next I asked him if the shoes alone were scary. With gentle encouragement, I took him to the hall to see the shoes where I had left them. I challenged him to talk about how the shoes could transform someone into a witch. "What if a man put them on?" "What if we painted them red?" I gave him control to find out how this could be less scary for him, and he had the idea he should put the shoes on! "Because," he said, "I know I am not a witch." He was able to see that they would not change me either. I was then able to put my shoes back on. At no time did I tell him he was silly or that big boys know better. (Levine, 2004, p. 1)

Provide Positive Attributes

When a child is stressed by feelings of being unlovable or disappointing, a teacher can be a priceless booster of self-confidence. You help a child feel that she or he is a good and worthwhile person every time you *comment with pleasure on specific actions* that show you really are noticing positive behaviors and accomplishments—even tiny ones (Honig, 2004a). When we use broad verbal brush strokes, such as "You are such a wonderful kid!" a child may feel uncomfortable. Children know that they sometimes make mistakes. They tend to feel uncomfortable with gushing adults, because they are worried that they cannot be perfect children all the time. Provide positive *specific* praise. Comment positively when a child moves over to let a peer sit on the bench next to him so that they can both do puzzles side by side. Give nurturing praise when a child helps carefully erase a blackboard. Specific positive attributes bolster a child's confidence. This is especially important if at home family members, who do not realize how stressful such comparisons are for a child, unfavorably compare that child with a brighter, prettier, or less mischievous sibling as they see it.

Spend One-to-One Time with a Worried Child

When children are worried, they cannot focus on play. They cannot focus on cooperating in classroom activities. Suppose Naffy, almost 3 years old, feels sad about his dad leaving him in the morning. After you have reassured the tot in a nurturing way, focus the child's attention on a fascinating activity. Pull up a basket of toy vehicles as the child sits snuggled next to you. Create an intimate game where the child makes many decisions, such as taking a trip to Florida. Disney World had enchanted him during his family's last vacation time. "If we want to take a trip to Disney World, what should we use to get there? Oh, you will take the train. Thanks for letting me know! And what do you think I will need to go along so that we can go traveling to Florida together? Oh. Thanks. That is a good idea you have that I should take the train, too. Once we get to Florida, what would you like us to plan to do first that you would *really* like to do?"

Socratic questions plus respectful and genuine deep involvement help the stressed child feel your special warmth and individual interest. This engagement is the secret key to the child's ability to accept the separation from his parents and relax, feeling secure in the world of child care.

LET THE CHILD TAKE THE LEAD
Telephone Talk

Keep a supply of toy telephones for conversations that a child initiates with a peer or adult. Children can initiate and also hang up whenever they want in these conversations. Often a child dictates what kind of conversation he or she wishes the caregiver to pursue. A 5-year-old during home visits asked me to play "wrong number." She was used to the regular game where she would pretend to dial the toy telephone and we would talk. After she was used to the game over many visits, then I decided that I would answer sometimes as if I were a butcher, or a hairdresser, or a zoo director, and tell her that she had reached a wrong number. She adored the feeling that she was in charge of the telephone game. "Play the wrong number game," she requested. She loved trying to explain to each wrong-number character I played in this game just whom she wanted to talk to and why.

Offer Specific Choices

Show genuine interest in the child's opinions when you see that a child is upset. Offering choices *gives children more control* over their decisions about own behaviors. If a child is having trouble settling on his cot at naptime and has been refusing to nap, quietly ask with real respect *which* side of the cot he prefers to lie down on before you snuggle his blanket around him.

Give a fussy child a choice between two solutions with which you are comfortable. This empowers each child as a decision maker, helps him to calm down, and leads to more cooperation. "Which would you prefer? Shall I toast your bread really dark? Or do you want me to toast it lighter before you spread the peanut butter and jelly?" "Which do you prefer today, syrup or honey on your pancakes?"

Teach an Indignant Child to Use an "I" Statement

Children with verbal skills will feel more powerful if they can say how they feel and why and what they want. "My toy!" is a firm way for a young toddler to assert himself and hang on to the truck he is playing with if a peer tries to tug it away. His verbalization is short, but it clearly states his wishes. A preschool child can say, "I was playing with the truck first" or, "I still need the blue crayon to finish my picture" or, "I don't like being pushed. Don't push me!" Rather than vaguely telling a complaining preschooler to go tell his classmate what he wants, teachers need to *model* and encourage children to use specific *"I" statements* when they feel intruded upon or stressed by peer behaviors.

Use the *I Can Problem-Solve* Program

Give power to a child to generate his or her solutions to a personal social problem by using the *I Can Problem-Solve (ICPS)* program. When there are troubles between peers, adults often suggest a reasonable way to calm the disagreement in the classroom. But does this always help the child think up his or her own solutions to a social problem? Shure (1992, 1994) suggested teaching a child how to figure out the *consequences* of inappropriate behavior. If a child is fighting with a peer over a toy or bullying a younger child, the adult helps the child to generate his or her own solution to social tensions with others. Shure's ICPS program provides teachers with tools to teach children the principles of problem-solving thinking. Children are challenged to think up their own alternatives to their social problem situations. The adult's role is to get the child to create possible alternative solutions, such as swapping a toy for the one he wants and has tried to hit out and grab from a peer. As a teacher, you are especially adept at being able to stimulate children to use thinking skills to solve emotional and social problems.

If a toddler comes toward you with a book he wants you to read immediately and knits his brow and clenches his fist in anger when he sees that you are very busy, then gently ask that child, "Can I read to you right *now* and also change Leanne's diaper *now*, at the same time?" You might promise him that *later*, as soon as you are finished diapering Leanne, you would love to read his book with him.

Ask questions that challenge little children to think about *consequences* when they are having social spats. "What might happen *next* if you keep pushing Jenny higher on the swing when she yells to let her slow down and get off?" "Is it a good idea to hit Greg to get him to play the doggie in your game, or is it not a good idea?"

Other ICPS concepts include *some of the time* versus *all of the time.* A preschooler might enjoy playing what Freddy wants some of the time but not all of the time. And, in turn, you can help Freddy understand that he probably wants to play what his friend suggests some of the time but not all of the time. You can also use the ICPS concepts of *before* and *after* to galvanize children's thinking skills. Tony hit Jim *after* Jim knocked down his block building. *Before* they can play with the tricycles outdoors, children need to work together to lug the tricycles out of the shed so that afterward they can enjoy riding. The same concepts will apply for smoothing a social conflict by suggesting that a child play what her friend wants to play *before* the friend plays the game she prefers.

Teachers who practice ICPS dialogues empower children with more emotional insights and socially appropriate interactions without telling the child in advance what the adult thinks is best. The sample game dialogue that follows (Shure & Spivack, 1978) was created for parent and child. It illustrates some of the ICPS concepts that stimulate children's emotional social thinking powers as they struggle to mediate between their own strong wishes and empathy for a peer's needs too.

Mother:	Robin, who hit you?
Child:	Natalie (a friend).
Mother:	What happened? Why did she hit you? (Mother elicits child's view of the problem.)
Child:	She just hit me.
Mother:	You mean she hit you for no reason? (Mother encourages child to think of causes.)
Child:	I hit her first.
Mother:	What for?
Child:	She won't let me look at her book.
Mother:	How did Natalie feel when you hit her? (Mother guides child to think of feelings of others.)
Child:	Mad.
Mother:	Do you know why she doesn't want you to look at her book? (Mother guides child to appreciate point of view of others.)
Child:	No.
Mother:	How can you find out?
Child:	I could ask her.
Mother:	See if you can find out. (Mother encourages child to seek facts and discover the problem.)
	(Later)
Child:	She said I never let her see my books.
Mother:	Now that you know why she said no, can you think of something you could do or say so she'll let you look at her book? (Mother encourages child to think of solution.)
Child:	I could stop playing with her.
Mother:	What might happen if you do that? (Child is guided to think of consequences of her solution.)
Child:	She might not be my friend.
Mother:	Do you want her to be your friend?
Child:	Yes.
Mother:	Can you think of something different to do so she'll still be your friend? (Mother encourages further solution thinking.)
Child:	I could let her have one of my books.
Mother:	That's a different idea. (pp. 121–122)

Notice that the child is encouraged to solve this frustrating social situation by her own problem solving. This technique takes patience and practice, but is a wonderful way to advance young children's abilities to deal with their own tensions arising from social conflicts. The more that children were encouraged daily by teachers to think about other ways to resolve their social spats, the fewer aggressive behaviors were tallied 3 months later (Shure & Spivack, 1978).

ICPS dialogues take practice, but they belong in every teacher's "social strategies tool kit" (Honig, 1996, p. 9). Their use will deeply gratify the adults who see increased classroom harmony as the result of persevering in daily use of the dialogues.

Listen to Bad Dreams to Defuse Children's Worries

Listening to a child's bad dreams can help alleviate a child's stress and worry. (Jalongo, 2003, p.124) provided a sample dialogue of how a teacher's genuine interest in the child's sharing his dream about a monster led to the child's introduction of less scary elements and to a peaceful resolution in his feelings.

Jeremy:	I had a dream about a monster.
Teacher:	Were you afraid?
Jeremy:	No, cause we be'ed friends. We played cards.
Teacher:	Let's make a picture of the monster.
Jeremy:	Okay. (while drawing)
Jeremy:	Here is the big fat monster's belly. This is his head. Here's his feet and his hair. There's his great, great big ears.
Teacher:	Where are you?
Jeremy:	I'm right down here . . . by the table. We played cards here. See these cards? These is monster cards. You have man cards.
Teacher:	What else did you do?
Jeremy:	We drank pop . . . in glasses.
Teacher:	Did you do anything else?
Jeremy:	We setted on a rocking chair.

Sharing nightmares or bad dreams with a calm, reassuring adult is a way for young children to get out the stress of the dream in the light of day and in the intimate company of a caring, genuinely interested adult.

CONCLUSIONS

This chapter provided a number of strategies that can work to calm children and increase classroom peacefulness. Singing songs and greeting each other in group care is a peaceful way to start the day and to help children feel a close bond with each other and with the teacher. It is important to provide soothing physical contact, admiring voice tones, and verbal reassurance, take the child's perspective, and provide opportunities and spaces for self-soothing. It can also be a good idea to let the child take the lead. Be accepting when children use a "lovey" for self-soothing. Using a child's name frequently and confirming positive attributes of a child enhances and promotes good feelings and self-esteem. Provide unobtrusive physical help, such as steadying a child's elbow, that will allow the child to experience the pleasure of completing a difficult structure, such as a block tower. The art of questioning and methods of promoting self-esteem were also discussed to provide guidance in soothing children and reducing stress.

STUDY QUESTIONS

What is a "lovey," and how can it work as part of a stress reducing technique for children?

How can you create a cozy retreat in your classroom? Why is it important to do this?

What are some ways you can reduce a child's stressors?

What is the *I Can Problem-Solve* program, and how can you use it in your classroom?

USING STRESS-REDUCING STRATEGIES WITH GROUPS OF CHILDREN

Many of the strategies teachers use involve working with groups of children rather than with an individual child. Teachers often use group times to teach cognitive concepts, such as big circle and little circle or red triangle and blue triangle. But group times can also be used to combine cognitive teachings and emotional teachings in order to promote more classroom peacefulness.

TEACH PRESCHOOLERS THE CONCEPTS OF *SAME* AND *DIFFERENT*

Four-year-olds are usually cognitively able to understand and apply the concepts of *same* and *different.* They exclaim indignantly that another child "has more cookies than me, Teacher!" Often, teachers work on cognitive exemplars to teach these concepts. They teach how shapes are different or the number of cheerios given to each child are the same or different. These two powerful concepts can also be used to decrease a child's emotional feelings of indignation and accusation when stressed in a peer altercation. Suppose a girl's friend does not want to play the game she prefers. A teacher says, "You want to play dolls and Sherry wants to build with blocks. She has a different idea from you. Sometimes you will want to play the *same game*. Now you have *different* ideas for play. Can you both figure out which game you could play first and which one you could play together afterward?"

Being able to master the concepts of same and different is essential for some children in order to understand aspects of turn taking, learning to share, and agreeing to play a game that was not their first choice.

A noncustodial father told me that his 3-year-old was complaining often during visits that he did not do things the way the boy's mom did them, including dressing him, preparing a meal, or giving him a bath. I suggested he use the concepts of *same* and *different* in an easy conversational tone to help the child become more comfortable with these differences. When they next went to the mall, the father took his little boy to different stores compared with those that Mom usually visited. When the boy complained, the father tried this technique. The little boy listened. This was something new to think about. Sometimes moms and dads do things, cook stuff, choose toys, read stories, and browse in stores the same way and sometimes in different ways. The boy seemed quite satisfied. He no longer complained when each parent behaved in his or her own special way.

This technique can work in child care not only to help children accept the ways in which group care differs from home care but also to help children become aware of and accept different cultural practices and customs in the families of their friends.

ENCOURAGE AND CREATE CONVERSATIONS WITH CHILDREN FROM DIVERSE BACKGROUNDS

Encourage conversations to help children share home experiences with one another. During mealtimes in particular children have a chance to become aware of different cultural and family styles.

In a very large center at lunchtime, each teacher sat with a group at a round table. A child frowned at her food and protested to the teacher, "That's not the way my momma serves hot dogs!" The teacher took advantage of this teachable moment. The child's protest offered an opportunity for her to go around the table asking all the children about the different ways their families served hot dogs. One preschooler said, "My dad lets us have mustard and ketchup on our hot dogs." Another pre-schooler said, "I like the hot dog by itself but I don't want to eat it in a bun the way my brother does." A child from a Latino family happily chimed in, "My mama gives me frijoles with my hot dog!"

Children heard about how their friends enjoy different ways of serving and eating foods. They became more comfortable with the idea that it is okay if children do not have exactly the same ways and eating routines at home and in child care. Tasting different foods and trying new ways of eating old favorites is a good opportunity for children to appreciate diversity.

Create conversations where children from diverse backgrounds share common preferences or worries. Children will interact more harmoniously the closer they feel to each other emotionally, despite coming from many different kinds of families or different cultural groups. Create commonalities. Talk with the children about their *common interests* and *common worries*. If children wake up from the roll of thunder in the nighttime when it is dark outside, what do they do? The children will feel closer to each other as they tell how they mostly want to get up from their beds and go to find their parents!

Ask about *common games* they enjoy. Children love to talk about favorite television programs, favorite outings, and favorite foods. They may decide after an animated talk that they all love pizza! Your genuine interest empowers them to chat together and feel closer emotionally to each other as they share their preferences. Keep sharing times safe, so that children share their ideas, preferences, remembrances, and enthusiasm without any fear of adult disapproval. You may choose to focus on specific topics, such as what they enjoyed on a trip to the zoo, a family picnic, or a visit with relatives. Children may want to share a story about a favorite cousin or friend with whom they play. Another topic might be, "What kind of animal would you like to be if you could turn into that animal for a little while?" Many preschoolers love to play being a kitty at dramatic play-time. If a child always names a predator, such as a shark or a monster tiger, this may indicate the child's uncertainty, or that he does not feel so secure.

HAVE A GROUP ASSEMBLY TO DEAL WITH AGGRESSIVE BEHAVIOR

When aggressive behaviors become too frequent in a classroom or a center, teachers can decide to hold a gathering with several groups of children. This can be a specific assembly to deal with the issue of aggression. The teachers can explain to the children that there seem to be too many times that children are trying to solve their problems by hitting, yelling, pushing, and snatching.

At such a meeting with the 4- and 5-year-olds at the Children's Center in Syracuse years ago, the teachers explained that hitting hurts. Teachers asked the children to think of ways that they could tell another child they were mad or upset without hitting or hurting. The teachers also explained, "When you feel frustrated (a word taught by using it to describe a child's upset feelings) and get mad at a playmate, you need to tell that child in words how you feel, what you want, or that you had the toy first and are still using it." The teachers also reminded the children that the adults were there to help them if they got into a disagreement with another child and that *children could call out for a teacher's help.*

A few weeks after the assembly, a teacher set out a big hunk of red playdough in the middle of the small table where two preschoolers were seated opposite one another, and the children were supposed to share together. One child in the teacher's class, Brad, felt exasperated when Janey, his play partner, kept pulling the large hunk of red playdough more and more toward herself. Brad's face clouded with anger that reflected his upset feelings. After the recent group dialogue, Brad, rather than reaching over and hitting Janey, yelled in loud indignation, "Teacher, Janey ain't sharing!" Teacher moved in quietly and reassuringly to restate rules.

Bullying and threatening other children sometimes happens in group care settings. Children who feel too many pressures and attempts to control their actions by adults at home may then try to control other children in class or on the playground. If they have been criticized a lot, children in turn may sneer or laugh at a peer's attempts at block building and threaten to knock it over. Sometimes when a child moves too close, then a peer might take this as a "threat" and act defensively, pushing aggressively. An older child in a mixed age group might use threats if he feels he can get needs met by scaring a younger child into doing just what the older one wants.

When he wanted to join a building project from which the children were strenuously excluding him, Alvin then moved in close to James and threatened, "My daddy is big and strong and he can beat up your daddy." James retorted, "My daddy has a bigger gun than your daddy."

Talk with the children at circle times and at an assembly about how threats make them feel. That is how other kids feel too. Ask the children to figure out other ways to handle conflicting wishes without threatening each other. If a child calls out "Alvin, I could beat up James for you!" don't feel discouraged. Remember that working to teach new ways to get rid of mad feelings is a learning experience that may be lengthier for some children. Clearly and calmly remind the children again that in their classroom the special idea is to find ways to settle troubles so that every child feels *cared about* (Kobak, 1979). Keep your determination to focus on finding ways to solve conflicts in peaceable ways. Kobak counsels that teachers must work toward increasing the *caring quotient* (CQ) in the classroom as well as children's IQ (intelligence quotient). Remind the children of the class goals. We are working together so that all the children feel that they are comfortable and can play peacefully in the classroom without feeling excluded or hurt. Work on increasing empathy and caring for others. Sometimes children learn empathy best by at first caring for a loved pet who whines when hungry. Understanding the feelings and needs of others is a long learning process in young children's lives.

For some group meetings, challenge the children's ability to think up their own solutions to emotional or social tussles by bringing up a *scripted* question. Ask each child for a suggestion that could resolve a particular problem between children. A problem to present might be one in which a teacher has wondered whether he or she should intervene or let the children struggle to resolve on their own.

Other problems might arise as a struggle between two playmates. Suppose Amy asks Jenna to borrow the sieve from her water tub and Jenna refuses to lend the sieve. What might Amy say so that Jenna will share? After sharing ideas, the children decide what will work best. Shure (1992) calls this technique "Pick the best; pick the worst." Children practice making decisions after they have generated many social solutions to a problem by then picking the best and worst solutions based on potential consequences for each decision.

TRY A SCRIPTED EMOTIONAL CURRICULUM

The Magic Circle Program provides curricular lessons for teachers who hold a special circle time each day when children are not judged for right or wrong answers or for their responses. For about 15–20 minutes per day teachers arrange seating for children in two concentric circles (Bessell & Palomares, 1970). The inner circle of children is going to participate in the Magic Circle talk that day. The outer circle may need more time to get comfortable with the talking process. This sequential program allows children gradually to learn to express emotions and tell stories about emotional events. The program starts with the children telling about something positive. Children tell about a time they did something that made another child happy or when another child did something to make them feel happy. The emotional curriculum moves gradually toward sharing more negative, stressful emotions, for example, when someone did something a child disliked, or when a child did something that made another child mad or sad. Children learn that they are safe to describe emotional events in the Magic Circle. There are no right or wrong answers, and real-life experiences are the center of the group meetings.

SET ASIDE SOME GROUP TIME TO TALK ABOUT FEELINGS

Acknowledge worrisome as well as welcome emotions. Young children need to learn words to express their feelings. Even young toddlers can learn the words *mad, sad,* and *happy* to describe some of their feelings. Preschoolers learn words for much more complicated feelings, such as *proud, worried, excited, patient, frustrated, embarrassed,* and *amazed.* It may seem as if children learn some negative feeling words more easily. "He's being mean, Teacher!" is heard quite early! We need to teach words so that children can as easily label peers as being helpful, generous, kind, sharing, and friendly.

In a second-grade classroom, a teacher held a daily circle time to encourage children to notice and report about their own positive behaviors or the actions of their classmates for that day. For each kind, caring action a child described, the teacher put a star up on a chart. After many hundreds of stars had been pasted, the children and the teacher celebrated with a small class party. In this study, the researchers also recorded prosocial actions of children randomly assigned to another class without the program. The researchers recorded similar levels of prosocial interactions for students in both classrooms prior to the program initiation. After many weeks of the program, participating children performed twice as many cooperative, sharing, and kind actions in the lunchroom, classroom, and the halls, compared with children from the control classroom (Honig & Pollack, 1990). The classroom climate becomes more peaceable when teachers make clear their positive endorsement and pleasure in peer-caring behaviors.

At group times you set aside for such talks, discuss thoughtfully the fact that everyone gets mad sometimes. Use the word *frustrated* with preschoolers. Then ask children to share times they got mad or frustrated—as when they tried hard to tie shoelaces but could not yet get the laces tied. Some children may share that they are very upset and angry when neighbors and relatives come to their home and fuss and coo over the new baby (Simon, 1974).

Every time children share a frustration or a situation that makes them mad, this is an opportunity for teachers. We gain precious insights into the inner emotional world of the children. When children share their stressed feelings, this gives adults a chance to create more effective ways to assist children with a specific problem.

What if a child tells the teacher that he is angry with a parent for yelling or punishing? At group-sharing time, a preschooler told in a resentful voice that his dad yelled at him when he was climbing on a high, narrow ledge. This kind of sharing provides a wonderful opportunity for you to help young children learn to reframe. What could be the parent's real deep-down feelings? The parent scolded loudly. But what was the dad's main feeling—angry or scared? The parent may have felt really worried that the child would fall and get hurt. Instead of communicating his worry, the adult yelled. Sometimes people yell when they are feeling angry. But sometimes they yell when they are worried. All of us need to learn to practice reframing skills! Sharing times, when children can talk about emotions, are a fine time to help children learn to think about the feelings of other people, including their parents, as well as their own feelings.

HONE YOUR TALENTS AS A TUNED-IN EMOTIONAL COACH

Help young children untangle surface angry feelings from the *underlying emotions* that may be responsible for stress. We need reminders that we serve children not just by enriching their cognitive learning but also by acting as effective emotional coaches. Of course, recognizing underlying emotions is not the same as being able to deal with stress in ways that reduce conflict or anger. But recognition of emotions, in others and in ourselves, is a first step on the long climb toward mature self-control. The ability to manage stressful emotions successfully is essential to reaching life goals (Goleman, 2006).

Try to Empathize with Outsized Child Fears

Adults need to sympathize with children's fears and yet not fall apart emotionally. It takes effort to stay calm and helpful when a child's stresses are severe. Adults may find it hard to grasp the despair a young child feels when that child imagines a threat of abandonment by a trusted person who is supposed to take care of him and keep him safe. Try to remember the terror you may have seen on the face of a crying little child even briefly separated from a parent in a crowded department store!

A 6-year-old boy had been living for several years in our community with his loving adoptive family. Each weekend, the family went to see how the construction workers were progressing at building their new house in a nearby suburb. When the house was finally finished, the parents announced to the little fellow with delight that they would be moving to the new house next week. The child burst into terrified tears. He sobbed out that if they were going to the new house, what would become of him? He told his folks that he did not know how to cook and take care of himself when left all alone in the house. How would he eat?

The 6-year-old's extreme distress reminds us of how important it is to *be very specific in explaining adult plans* to young children. Their cognitive abilities may not be up to understanding what seem like trivial bits of social information, such as the concept that when families move to a new house, then all the people in the family move together.

Be specific and use simple words in explaining a hassle or a worry to a child. We need to be so clear and specific when talking with little children. Adults often expect that children will understand what is happening when they hear grown-ups talk. I was on a home visit once when the mom talked on the phone with her husband about when he was going to be home for dinner and nodded as she listened to his reply; she then turned to her preschooler and said, "Well, daddy's not going to be home for dinner. He's all tied up at the office!" The little boy broke into terrified tears. From watching television programs, he assumed that thugs had bound up his poor daddy with ropes and were holding him prisoner.

Feel proud of your special skill as an *emotional coach*. Stay aware of differences in stresses that affect each child and in the ability of each child to manage personal or group stress.

CARRY OUT TENSION-RELEASING BODY EXERCISES DURING CIRCLE TIME

Tensions flow out of our bodies as we pay specific attention to each part of our body that is tense. Often an adult remarks, "That guy is a pain in the neck!" But this may not be only symbolic! Difficult interpersonal interactions sometimes do result in physical neck stiffness and pain. When aggravated, people often feel pains physically.

Use Relaxation Games in Circle Time to Reduce Stress

Seat the children, barefooted and with enough space between each child, in a circle with feet stretched out facing the inside of the circle. First ask them to wiggle and then relax the toes on each foot. Then ask them to rotate ankles slowly until their ankles feel all relaxed. Ask the children to push out with their heels and curl their toes toward them. They will feel their calf muscles stretch. Ask each child to sit with knees bent and soles touching. Then bend forward with the children. Thigh muscles stretch in this exercise. Keep going to help tensions flow out of each muscle group as you travel upward through the body, asking children to tense and relax muscles. Tummy muscles can be sucked in and then pushed outward.

Ask children to stretch their arms out forward in front of them slowly as far as they can reach. Have them to try to touch toes with their palms facing downward. Then, with palms facing upward, have them raise and lower their arms ten times. Then have them slowly reach arms around and clasp hands in back of the head with elbows, hugging the head. Ask the children to fan out their elbows and stretch their elbows slowly like flapping elephant ears. As they do ten flaps back and forth, they will feel the stretch in the muscles under the arms. They will feel other muscles as they stretch their arms parallel to each other behind their backs. Then their arms can be gently brought down to rest, one on each thigh. Tell them to breathe slowly for a while.

Another time, when children are sitting in a circle, ask them to practice clenching one fist at a time. Tighter. Even tighter! Now relax that fist. This isometric exercise often helps an older child find a way to control a clenched fist rather than using it right away to hit out at a child who has made an aggravating remark. Sometimes a child who has felt aggravated by teasing finds this exercise helpful if he or she puts the hand in a pocket and clenches the fist tightly before relaxing, rather than impulsively using that fist to punch out when teased by a classmate.

Wrists can be rotated. Fingers can be wiggled, although wiggling a pinkie and keeping the other fingers still is a hard job. Children will be amazed at how many muscles they can control. Usually little children boast, "Teacher, feel my muscle. See how strong I am." Somehow the upper arm muscle seems to be the one that indicates power and strength for them. Now they are finding that they can be in charge of moving a lot of other body muscles.

When the children are sitting quietly, encourage them to let their shoulders droop a bit to relax. They can breathe in and out slowly with droopy shoulders, pretending they are like rag dolls. Practice rotating each shoulder, one at a time, to let go of any tense feelings. Now each child swivels, so that the children are seated facing each other's backs rather than inward toward the middle of the circle. This gives each child room to stretch each arm outward, to the left and right. Pretend that they are all shaking crabby feelings and worries out from each arm and hand. Ask the children to pretend that as they shake their arms and fling the worries away, the worries are flying away from them.

Go slowly as you proceed with face and neck exercises. Rotate the head from front to the right and back again several times and then to the left. Each person slowly rolls the head all the way around until it comes back to the front. Children can feel the head relax as it drops forward after a full rotation.

The children may well enjoy wriggling noses and making faces with lips. Help the children find a way to smooth the forehead. All of the group can feel with their palms how they are smoothing out imaginary worry wrinkles from the forehead. Practice together a grin and a smile. Practice together making a frown. Have the children noticed that a deep crease between the eyes is a sign of worry or anger? Let each child make a pretend frown line between the eyes and then use their palms to smooth out those forehead frown lines.

Children feel more secure with predictable, pleasurable routines. They will look forward to circle times for tensing and relaxing muscles as a special activity that allows them to control their own body parts. If you add rhythmic chants to some of the exercises, children may find them even more pleasurable.

Even when school lesson plans in a classroom do not allow much time for body relaxation exercises, encourage children daily to do eye massage. Close the eyes and massage the skin around the eyes gently in slow circles. In many schools in China, I observed how relaxing this daily exercise was for school children seated at their desks.

End exercise-relaxation time by having each child lightly massage the scalp with gentle hands, so that the last of the tension gremlins can fly up and away. Tensions in life will certainly surface again. Having practiced slow, easy exercises, children will feel empowered to know how to get rid of tense body feelings themselves in comfortable ways that they practice together with your guidance. They become more assured as they control tension and relaxation of their own muscles.

Dance During Circle
Time to Relax Tensions

Relaxation movements are not the only way to unwind the body. Dancing does wonders. Choose slow skating waltzes and other dancing music for toddlers to relax, twirling dreamily to slow tunes. Some preschoolers love lively and stomping music. They jump and leap as they dance to those strong beats. Watch the children as they dance. Tensions flow out of their bodies as they move to the music.

ACCEPT THE AWESOME
PHYSICALITY OF YOUNG CHILDREN

Often young children let go of stressed feelings better when adults let go of stressed feelings about children's energetic needs to romp about. In modern Disney tales based on A. A. Milne's classic Christopher Robin stories, Tigger bounces a lot! His high-energy bouncing surely exasperates his friends, when he bounces smack in the middle of friend Rabbit's baskets of carefully gathered vegetables and scatters them about. Yet Tigger is a beloved and good friend. The animals talk about what they should do. They decide to shun him until Tigger learns not to bounce. When they won't play with him, Tigger feels so sad and upset. He and his friends really do care for each other. The other animals reconsider. They decide to accept Tigger's bounciness rather than stay angry at their friend's high-energy bouncing.

PROVIDE SAFE SPACES
FOR VIGOROUS MOVEMENT

Youngsters between the ages of 5 and 16 need to be active up to 2 hours a day. This advice comes from the European Heart Study (Anderson, et al., 2006) with almost 3,000 children. During outdoor play, researchers attached a small machine to children's hips to record accelerations in body movement. The children who were more active than others had healthier readings for blood pressure, cholesterol, and insulin regardless of child obesity. Be sure to plan outdoor play to decrease physiological indices of stress for children. Even in winter weather, on a sunny day when they are warmly dressed, children enjoy outdoor play. They play King of the Mountain on high piles of snow at the back of a playground. In hot climates, parents can pitch in and create shade awnings over a play yard to protect children from too much sun.

Attuned to temperament traits, you notice that some children in your group have particularly high activity needs. High activity needs are more likely to get children into difficulties with classmates. Your creative ingenuity provides ways for high-energy children to move vigorously to let off steam. Place a sturdy rocking horse in a corner in the toddler room. Then high-energy toddlers know where to run to rock with enormous pleasure and vigor when the need arises.

If a high-energy child comes near, take both hands and with a broad smile offer to play a jumping game. Hold hands with the preschooler as he tries to jump higher and higher in place. In the gym, provide enough tricycles, tumbling mats, hobbyhorses, and climbing equipment for children who calm down best when you arrange safe physical activities for them.

> After his parent left in the morning, I asked Wally, a young preschooler, who seemed somewhat upset at his mom's leaving, if he wanted me to read him a story. "One," I thought I heard him say. "Oh, you want one book?" I smiled at him. "No, won!" he corrected me urgently. What he wanted to do was run and run for a long while! But he could not yet pronounce the letter *r*, a difficult phoneme (sound) for many toddlers.

Kids can provide lots of amusing anecdotes as we try to figure out ways to get them through stresses that they may be feeling.

CHOOSE ACTIVITIES TO ENHANCE SELF-ESTEEM

Young children often feel powerless and need teachers to enlarge their perceived spheres of control. Babies cannot manage wrist control to get a spoon full of cereal to the mouth. Toddlers struggling with articulation have trouble making themselves understood by adults. Preschoolers become frustrated trying to tie shoelaces.

Children do not choose their care placements. Even when demanding, they may not get the intimate loving adult attention they crave. They have no control if parents decide to have a younger sibling close in age to them. Indeed, for many years they have little control over anal and urethral sphincters! Feelings of lack of control serve as an important ingredient that fuels some child tensions. Little kids often burst out, "You are not the boss!" when a strange adult asks them to behave. Children sometimes act defiant when they are desperately trying to hold on to a sense of having some control in their lives. This is especially true if a child lives in a household with rigid rules. Muscle-relaxing exercises can help children feel more in control of their own bodies. Brainstorm other techniques that can help and share these with co-workers during in-service sessions.

Create and Encourage Nurturing Scenarios Using Toys

In the classroom dramatic corner, provide toy cribs or cardboard boxes that can serve as cribs for dolls and teddy bears. Parents may want to pitch in and provide blankets for bassinets for baby bears. Create scenarios with the children. Baby bear has a tummy ache. Or dolly is really tired today. Maybe she has a fever or a sore arm from a shot at the doctor's. Encourage the children to care tenderly for each toy animal or doll (Figure 1). Praise them for taking such good care of a sick teddy that may have a broken arm in a sling and needs a child's special gentle care in settling onto his cot for a nap.

Figure 1.   An example of a little girl nurturing her doll.

Set up water tables where toddlers can tenderly bathe their rubber dolls. Protect clothes with a plastic smock. Keep a sponge mop handy for the floor. Notice how your children get into doll washing! They soap up their babies, rinse them off, and pat them dry with elaborate care. Water play is always soothing, whether at the beach or in the playroom. Combining water play with nurturing a dolly is a wonderful way to unwind. Be sure to provide girl and boy dolls representing different cultural groups.

Dig in the Earth: Plant Flowers and Vegetables

Encourage children to nurture plants and classroom creatures. The world of the outdoors provides opportunities for nurturing growing creatures as well as romping about. Bird feeders must be filled. Plants must be tended. In warm climates where hummingbirds live, the children will look on in awe if a hummingbird comes to sip sugar syrup from a feeder. Plant butterfly bushes to attract butterflies—often called "flying jewels." In colder climates, look into installing a bird feeder that attaches directly outside on a windowsill. The children will press fascinated noses against the pane as birds come to peck at the seed the children have set out.

Dig holes to create deep beds to plant flowers and vegetables in an outdoor garden plot. Digging will both energize and calm children as they work together. Tending to their flower or plant gives children pride and awe as the plants grow. Caring for creatures in the classroom evokes tenderness. Grow potato vines in the classroom. Digging, planting, weeding, watering—children absorbed in caring activities will have fewer body tensions. Most of the children will have watched Mr. Rogers feed his fish daily on television. Now they too have a chance to nurture living creatures, including plants, hamsters, and wild birds at the feeders.

MODEL THAT IT IS OKAY TO MAKE MISTAKES SOMETIMES

Some children are scared to try an art activity if they have been scolded for getting clothes messy. They strongly refuse to squeeze cornstarch goop or spread finger paint. Some even draw back their hands as if frightened at what adults might say if hands get squishy or sticky in an activity.

Some children have difficulties with motor processing skills. Suppose people have criticized a child as clumsy when she tried an activity such as hitting a big ball with a lightweight bat. It is important that young children realize that we all make mistakes while we are learning new skills. Even after grown-ups learn something, such as how to keep a low flame under chocolate pudding and keep stirring while it is cooking, they might forget if distracted. Then the pudding turns out lumpy and even burned on the bottom.

If you forget a politeness rule and a preschooler reminds you, cheerfully say, "You sure are right, honey. That is a good rule, and I need to remember it!" Once when I yawned, a preschooler informed me that I needed to cover my mouth when I yawn. That is her mommy's rule! And I agreed with her that it was a good rule for politeness. Making a mistake is not a sin like uncaring or hurting behavior. Little children may not be aware of the difference between making legitimate mistakes because we have not yet learned a skill very well or we do not know a bit of information and intentionally breaking the rules. A toddler might call a sheep a doggie. This mistake is far different from hurting others' feelings or hurting them physically. Children need to get comfortable with the reality that from time to time we all make mistakes.

I went on a home visit while Mom was away and Grandma was caring for the toddler, who did not have on shoes or socks as the day was warm. He enjoyed very much the game of "This little piggy went to market; this little piggy stayed home; this little piggy had roast beef; this little piggy had none. And this little piggy went 'Wee, wee, wee all the way home.'" He grinned broadly and asked to play the game several times. However, when his mom returned, he informed her that the nice lady had played good games with him, but that she had made a "big mistake"! Apparently he and Mom were vegetarians, and they always used the word *tofu* instead of *roast beef* while playing that lovely game.

We need to grin and we surely gain more insights into early childhood from some of our own mistakes.

KEEP CLASSROOMS ORDERLY AND HARMONIOUS IN PEACEFUL WAYS

Do not confuse messiness with chaos. Certainly, toys get scattered on the floor. But there are times when children can be calmed by the orderliness of a classroom. Fiese (2006) showed children pictures of family scenes with messy kitchens and dinner tables. Some of the kitchen pictures she showed reflected orderliness in table settings with kitchen utensils and things neatly stored in their place. Research revealed that children felt more secure and decided that families were happier and getting along better when things looked orderly.

FEED KIDS REGULARLY

Young children act crabby and stressed when they are hungry. Every child is different in how much the tummy can hold. Some infants need to nurse every 2 hours. Others can go 3 or 4 hours between feedings. An empty tummy results in a cranky child without an adult always realizing where the distress is coming from. Set out nutritious snacks that offer choices for children. Some young children have difficulty getting used to the textures of some foods. If children participate in setting the table for eating, they will feel proud of their skills at making their eating spaces prettier and being such good helpers. They feel proud that they can pour juice or milk by themselves from a small plastic pitcher. They can spread their own peanut butter and jelly on a whole-wheat cracker. Food is a wonderful way to decrease stress for children and adults alike. Be sure you serve healthful snacks that are available for generous periods of time both morning and afternoon.

Compulsive overeating is another stress sign caregivers want to watch for. A 4-year-old's dad, when he had his child with him on weekends, kept him in diapers for the pleasure of still taking care of a young child. His mom was trying to help him learn toileting skills. The child overate ravenously as his way to cope with his bewilderment; he lived with conflicting parental expectations.

Overeating can be a sign of stress just as continuous food refusal alerts teachers to child stress. Serotonin, a neurotransmitter and a major target of antidepressant drugs, makes people feel good. Comfort foods such as dark chocolate increase serotonin. Cortisol and insulin production are stepped up in a person's body when there is chronic stress. This causes the appetite to increase and can lead to a child's overeating high-calorie fats and sweets. One anxious child, wanting only "perfect" grades in school, was a very picky eater and only nibbled at home. But the parents noticed that their (supposedly) hidden stores of candy in the kitchen closets were often depleted! Attitudes and behaviors with foods can indicate child stress. Therapists report that some disturbed children who have been abused or neglected will hoard food compulsively, even when generously fed in a safe, new environment.

KEEP NAP TIMES
SOOTHING AND SERENE

Sufficient sleep is a genuinely wonderful stress buster! Soft music, leisurely back rubs as children are lying on their cots, snuggly blankets, and dim lights promote restfulness. You have probably noticed that children who do not rest well at naptime are often less able to settle into classroom routines and into harmonious peer play later in the afternoon.

CELEBRATE RITUALS

Predictability is an important curricular ingredient that lessens child anxiety. Young children have hazy concepts of time. They assure a teacher that "Grandma is coming next week for my birthday" although the birthday is months away. I once asked a group of preschoolers at the lunch table what we would be doing after lunch. Of course, every day after lunch, we washed up, brushed teeth, got onto cots with blankets, and settled in for naptime. "We going to the zoo, teacher?" one child asked animatedly. "We going out to the playground!" happily announced another. Predictable patterns to the day increase child security even as they increase child awareness of how activities are planned and sequenced in time.

Most teachers have special rituals for a child's birthday. This might be a good time to go around the table where goodies are set out and ask each child to tell the birthday child something nice about the child on his or her special day. Use morning greeting rituals to help children come together as a group before they each choose an interesting play activity. Special songs that signal time to put away toys or time to use inside voices are rituals that keep calmness during the day.

INVOLVE CHILDREN AS ADMIRED
AND APPRECIATED CLASSROOM HELPERS

Praise children for their specific helping behaviors. Involved in activities that further the comfort and orderliness of their living space, young children feel safe and secure in their families and classrooms. They feel so important! They feel so proud of their grown-up abilities to organize and make their environment happier, more pleasant, and less likely to lead to stress compared with living in a chaotic space with toys tossed all around. Preschoolers will do chores far more cheerfully when *adults work helpfully alongside them* and admire their contributions. Empower children by engaging them in discussing helpful chores needed to keep the classroom a happy place. Preschoolers will especially enjoy being part of the planning process. They may decide that they need more space for block play or for the indoor climber. They may suggest more convenient arrangements for storing the blocks. When you work at clean-up time with a child who acts discouraged and gives up easily, your quiet presence, low reassuring voice, and helpfulness decrease that child's distress and increase feelings of competence.

Involve children in planning special occasions such as a visit by parents. They can bake cookies ahead of time. They can decide what table will contain their clay work and where they prefer their painting and collage artwork to be exhibited.

PREPARE CHILDREN FOR CHANGE

Children are less anxious when adults are specific about plans. The unknown, the unanticipated, or the unfamiliar easily upset some children. The more clearly teachers and caregivers spell out *what* will happen, *when* it will happen, and *how* it will happen, the less stressed some children feel. It is interesting that teachers do this when preparing for a possible fire drill at child care. They give careful, clear directions. They show children just where and what will happen. Notice how a child who refuses to put his paper plate from lunch in the garbage pail will act much less upset and cooperate more if told exactly what will happen next and why. "See, our hands are all messy with sticky sauce from our macaroni and cheese. So now we will need to go and get our hands washed." Talk clearly. Speak slowly. Explain in small phrases.

Prepare children for future happenings with simple, matter-of-fact words spoken in a reassuring voice. This will decrease any feelings of uncertainty that can lead to negativisms and refusals. Question children gently if they seem particularly worried. Once at our center we made a plan to take our preschoolers to visit the local airport. One little fellow acted absolutely frightened and said he would *not* go on that planned trip. It turned out that he had never seen an airplane on the ground. Teachers had told the group that during our planned visit, the nice people at the airport would take us to visit the inside of a plane. This young preschooler believed that the planes he saw flying way up in the sky would be too small to fit into. He was terrified that he would be squashed if we made him go into an airplane. Sometimes children's stress can be fixed by simple, clear descriptions and reassurances.

GIVE CHILDREN REASONS FOR BEHAVIORS EXPECTED IN THE CLASSROOM

Suppose a toddler crows with joy as he laboriously climbs up on a table in the room. He is upset because you ask him nicely to get down. As you help him down, explain that the table is for putting out snacks at snack time. The table needs to be clean. "Down you go. I am helping you down. You could tumble off a table. Now you can play nice and safe on the floor." You may have to explain many times why children have to hold on to the banister in the child care center if they are walking downstairs to visit the cook or another classroom. Stress is lessened when children feel that requests are reasonable. Magic markers are for coloring on paper; they are not for marking on the wall. "Let's go get a sponge and some water in a basin to clean off the marks. Then I will bring you paper to draw on." If a child is bothering a peer, speak for the child who is being upset. "Jerry does not like you to run your truck over his back when he is lying down. You can have a good drive with your truck on the floor."

PROVIDE UPBEAT, POSITIVE EMOTIONAL FEEDBACK TO CHILDREN WHEN POSSIBLE

Care providers, whether teachers or parents, are models for children. Do the adults in the child's life tend to scream, yell, throw things, physically assault, or jeer at others? Do the adults model acceptance of some unexpected nuisance events? When a child spills fruit juice that splashes all over, does the teacher calmly get sponges and ask all to help to clean up? How and what adults teach children to do with angry feelings is very important. How does the teacher react on entering the bathroom and finding that a toddler has stuffed the sink with paper towels and it is overflowing? Think about scenarios that could have been stressful for the children and yourself that you handled with grace and aplomb. Think about times you spoke positively and cheerfully to children, even when the tower of blocks fell down or they felt so frustrated and mad that they could not make a toy work the way they wanted to. *Endorphins* are neurotransmitters that improve mood in persons young and old. On the contrary, *stress hormones* increase when thoughts and feelings are angry or scared. *Optimistic feelings and talk encourage a cascade of endorphins.* Provide daily doses of upbeat talk and cheerful remarks to encourage children. They gain more energy to cope with stress. You are providing a model of how to handle mild or difficult stressful situations with aplomb and soothing language strategies. Be proud of the model you give to the children!

DO NOT IGNORE AGGRESSIVE INTERACTIONS

Teachers often have to make challenging decisions about when to intervene in upsetting situations between children. For a small disagreement, often if a teacher waits a minute or so children on their own solve their own problems. Outdoors on the snowy playground, Jacki, a younger child, called out that he wanted to build a snowman with the older preschoolers. At first they feared that he would mess up their snowman building, and they refused to let him join in. Jacki, a resourceful child, then offered to help them pull the wagon back and forth between the heaps from which they were scooping their snow and the site where they were building the snowman. However, when children are kicking, punching, and hurting each other, then ignoring the aggression only leads to escalations.

> Four-year-old Dina came home and announced to her parents that it was okay to hit. Her father and mother were surprised and questioned her. Dina informed her mom that Mr. Jerson, her teacher, did not care if kids fought. He ignored the hitting and did not do or say anything. Thinking about this, Dina, an astute observer of life in her classroom, concluded that if hitting was okay according to the teacher, then the kids could hit each other whenever they wanted to.

Helping children deal with angry feelings without attacking others requires a lot of sleuthing work and ingenuity from teachers. Some techniques work *some* of the time with some children. The more a caregiver helps children feel very safe and personally loved in the classroom, the more that child is likely to listen to suggestions about how to handle anger without hurting others. Create an imaginary (but psychologically available) personal game bag of stress-reducing techniques that you can choose from in each challenging situation (Honig, 2003b). One teacher, while smiling, may use a very low voice tone as if a loving growly bear was asking the children to listen. Another teacher might have a special finger wiggle that alerts the children that the noise level is getting too high for the group. Another teacher sometimes bursts into a loud Broadway senti-mental tune to get the group's attention. Another example is a teacher who calls out "Si'l vous plait!" in French to startle the children into giving her the attention she needs for teaching the lesson.

BAKE "GET OUT THE MAD" COOKIES

Fred Rogers (popularly known by generations of children as Mr. Rogers) believed that one of the most important jobs of a parent was to help a child find healthy ways to deal with anger. He expressed this focus by asking, "What do we do with the mad that we feel?" (Rogers & Sharapan, n.d.). One of the activities he suggested was to bake "get out the mad" cookies with the angry child. He reassures kids that the cookies taste bet-ter the more they are pounded. The recipe is available at the PBS Kids web site under Mr. Rogers (http://pbskids.org/rogers/parentsteachers/theme/1691.html).

Any baking activity where children can mush, squeeze, pound, and roll dough could prove deeply satisfying at allowing children to get out angry feelings. Children use their tense muscles in creative ways to make baked goodies that smell delicious during baking and taste delicious when ready to eat! In some classrooms where Jewish children are attend-ing, the children all bake challah bread for their parents on Fridays. Fragrance, ritual, and the pleasure of kneading and braiding dough all contribute to a sense of purpose and peacefulness. If baking is not an option in your facility, let the children squeeze and pound playdough or clay. As children poke, pull apart, and knead playdough or shape it into long snakes or dragons, they not only express their artistic creativity but also let off steam from problems bothering them. Smashing and smooshing clay or playdough is a therapeutic, safe, wordless way to express frustrations.

SLOW DOWN YOUR PACE
TO EASE SOME TRANSITION-TIME TROUBLES

Children hate to be rushed. They like to eat at their own pace. Be flexible. Some of your little ones can get down from the lunch table and play while others are still eating. Some children eat so much more slowly than others. Some children get really upset if hurried to finish and clean up after eating or playing.

QUICKEN YOUR PACE FOR OTHER TRANSITION TIMES

Waiting patiently for lunch or a chance to go outside is hard for young children. Squirmy and cranky, some children will start shoving and pushing others if they have to wait a long time in a line while teachers struggle to help put on each child's winter clothing. They get restless and droopy when forced to sit still at a table when food service is delayed for quite a while. Not all children are suddenly ready to use indoor voices quietly as they come back to their rooms after noisy outdoor play. Some teachers are skilled at making a game of helping children make the transition from outdoor play to quieter steps and voices while coming back in the classroom. They ask children to put on imaginary earphones. Rather than shushing or criticizing boisterous, bouncy running into the building, they ask the children to pretend to listen to special dreamy outer space music while coming back inside.

Reassure children during transitions from indoor to outdoor play that their work will be safe if they are worried about complying with your request to change activity.

> Martin was busy building a tall tower and it was his group's time to go out to the playground. When the teacher announced that it was time to go to the playground, Martin frowned in anger. Rather than have him say "No!" loudly and stubbornly, the teacher took time to acknowledge his wonderful building. She promised that his construction would remain safely there for him to work on when recess time was over.

Teachers are adept at using creativity in such situations. They ease transition-time woes for young children often by singing silly songs or tapping rhythms together on the table. What kinds of silly songs do you make up and sing together while waiting for food at the lunch table? "We're waiting for our fried worms and chocolate-covered ants. We're waiting for some fried worms and gooey ants for dessert!" Preschoolers who are used to humorous games may grin and chime in with their own ideas for bizarre edibles!

USE HUMOR

Laughter is good for the heart and for encouraging cascades of endorphins. Watching a comedy increases blood flow, which decreases if we watch a movie with lots of mayhem. Humor eases caregiver stress too. Suppose you have just finished cleaning up a toddler in a highchair but forgot to take his dish from the highchair tray. Then you look back to see that he has dumped the rest of the vegetable soup in his bowl all over his hair. Tell yourself that a vegetable shampoo and facial would cost a fortune in a swanky spa! A humorous take on some child mishaps, which might be exasperating to hardworking caregivers, reflects good *reframing skills*, reduces the stress of the situation, and even gives it a humorous feel. Such an episode will make a good story to laugh about with friends later on.

Tell silly jokes that the children can giggle at from time to time. A toddler teacher sitting at snack table with her children said with a big grin: "Oh, yummy. I am going to eat up my snack. And then I think that I will eat up Jenny's and then Louie's snack too, and then all the snacks!" At first the children looked worried. Then Louie piped up with dawning realization and a relieved big smile on his face: "Teacher, you joking!" The teacher smiled broadly and they all had a good laugh together.

Laughter releases tension. Children who are happy in their lives smile and laugh a lot more than worried or angry children. Tell corny jokes. Even toddlers who do not get the conceptual incongruities in jokes love the humorous format. They giggle and roll on the floor when you tell knock-knock jokes. Preschoolers want to chime in and add outrageously silly answers to, "Why did the chicken cross the road?" jokes. They love easy-to-understand silly jokes: "How could you stop a dog from barking in the back seat of the car? Put him in the front seat!" "What goes woof-woof, tick-tock? A watch dog!"

Younger toddlers carry out jokes via physical humor. A toddler thrusts her bare toes into an empty round oatmeal cardboard box and grins, "Shoe!" Toddlers give absurd names to familiar creatures or objects and enjoy creating humorous exchanges.

Two-year-old Shoshannah came near my chair and said, "Grandma Alice, you're Sobaka!" (her family's dog). Playing along with her mischievous grin, I said with a smile, "And you are Tasha!" (the name of her other grandma's dog). Shoshannah giggled with joy; we continued the back-and-forth game of attributing names she knew of assorted doggies belonging to relatives and friends.

Older toddlers and preschoolers express humor sometimes by extending a pattern of words to absurd lengths (Bergen, 2006).

> When C. was finishing eating lunch, Mother said she was going to the store and he could come too. He said, "And C. can come too, and Dad can come too, and Fluffy can come too, and cheese can come too, and bread can come too. (p. 148)

Older children love jokes with tongue-twister words or words with double meanings, as in the riddle: "Question: How come you can never starve to death in a desert? Answer: Because of the sand which is there!" (Honig, 1988 p. 69).

When a day is dreary and children seem somewhat droopy or out of sorts, try grinning at them and making requests that they soon learn are *teacher sillies*. "Can you smile with your toes?" "Can you make your fingers giggle?" "Can you show me how you laugh with your elbows?"

USE CHANTS AND RHYMES TO INCREASE LEARNING PLEASURE

Sensitivity to the needs of children coming from many different cultures in our schools challenges us to make learning enjoyable for young children whose primary language is not English. When children are learning English as a second language in the early grades, teachers find humorous rhymes and chants a happy way to assist them to enjoy their adventures in learning a new language. The Letter People program turns each letter of the alphabet into a fun character. Smiling at the images they conjure, the children chant, "Mr. B. has beautiful buttons" or "Mr. M has a munching mouth." Amusing rhyming chants help decrease anxious feelings and make learning a more enjoyable experience. Teacher use of rhythms, songs, funny rhymes, and vivid images decreases tense feelings that some children have when they are learning something new and puzzling in class.

ENCOURAGE IMAGINATION

In the "Magic School Bus" series, the teacher Ms. Frizzle takes the children on wild, unbelievable journeys to other planets and under the sea. Children do love safe routines they are familiar with and count on. But once they feel secure in child care they will love creatively conceived special events. Imaginative situations provide welcome relief for a class on dreary days when the weather outside is miserable and the feelings inside match the weather. This might be a day to prepare an imaginary picnic. Spread out a large green sheet to become a pond of water. Announce a special picnic by the "waterside" for lunchtime. Let the children pitch in to make peanut butter and jelly sandwiches or other foods. Encourage them to arrange cloths in baskets to carry on their arms as they stroll with their picnic fixings to a space near the pretend expanse of green water that the sheet represents. Fill a shallow plastic play pool with sand and set it near the green sheet. Provide small pails and shovels. Hide some tiny plastic dinosaurs in the sand. After the picnic and the clean up, the children extend their imaginative play near the pretend pond. They dig in the sand to find the dinosaurs. Creativity is a uniquely human treasure. Creative activities can be counted on as tension busters (Honig, 2001).

USE ART ACTIVITIES TO REDUCE TENSIONS

Art activities are a way for children to express their feelings. A child takes a drippy brush and watches with wide eyes, entranced as the blue paint gently slides down the easel page in a long blue blob. Given collage materials, children arrange and paste colorful sprinkles, bits of torn paper, and stickers all over a sheet of paper. Their faces reflect their absorption in artwork and their deep appreciation of their own creations. Artwork permits sad emotions to emerge also. Lonnie drew a bus and then scribbled all over it with a brown marker. The teacher was puzzled. She did not act disappointed by his scribbles. She did ask him gently to tell her about his picture. The child soberly explained, "That is the ambulance that took my dad to the hospital." The brown scribbles over Lonnie's picture expressed his dark scared feelings about his father's illness.

A child worried about his divorced parents' quarrels drew a picture for his counselor of Mom and Dad on opposite ends of the paper. He drew each with long arms that he joined together in the middle of the piece of paper. His dearest longing was that his two parents would make peace and hold hands together.

KEEP A PEACE ROSE

Keep a Peace Rose, a flower made of silk, in a pretty and unbreakable vase in the classroom (Paulson, 1997). If two children are fighting over a toy, over a role in dramatic play, or over who has a turn first, then set up a routine to use the Peace Rose. One of the children goes over and gets the Peace Rose. Whoever holds the rose may tell what has happened, how she or he feels about that, and what she or he thinks should be done about the situation. After that, the other child gets a turn to hold the rose and say how she or he really feels and what happened. The rules about use of the Peace Rose do not allow children to call each other names. The children must interact directly with each other to solve their social interaction problem (Honig, 1999). When they finish expressing their feelings and their take on the disagreement, the children come to some way to resolve the problem. Then they both say, "We declare peace." A teacher may ask a child who comes to complain about a stressful social situation in the classroom, "Do you feel that you need to go get the Peace Rose?"

USE PUPPETS TO ENHANCE CHILD PARTICIPATION

Puppets are an ancient art that entrances children who watch social violence in this safe theatrical form. In French parks, young children watch puppet theatres with rapt attention as puppet figures yell at and bop each other in classic skits. But puppets can also be used to teach more peaceable ways of resolving conflicts. Create puppet characters such as Homer Helper and Fannie Fixer to add interest to your talks with the children about how we can be helpers when a peer acts upset. Puppets will be more interesting to some children than just talking about caring for each other in the classroom. Puppet use increases children's interest in ways to promote kindness, sharing, and helping behaviors. The more peaceable the children's interactions, the less stressful the climate of the classroom will be.

ENCOURAGE SELF-CONTROL AS AN ONGOING TASK

Have the children in your classroom learn a bunch of self-control techniques, such as walking away from a threatening peer or telling that peer in words how mad they feel. Do they lunge physically and attack when they feel angry? Do they cry hard? Do they smash toys in response to angry feelings? Teachers use their finely tuned observational skills to figure out where to begin to teach self-control skills to stressed children with low threshold tolerance for getting mad quickly. Teachers soon learn what each child's stress threshold is. They become familiar with each child's behavioral style in response to anger, scary feelings, peer rejections, and other frustrations.

WATCH FOR AND REJOICE IN THE WAYS THAT CHILDREN HELP HEAL EACH OTHER'S HURTS

As children enter into play scenarios they themselves create, they spontaneously invite other children to play roles in their scenarios. Even an isolated child might find herself or himself responding to a peer's play scenario and agree to take on a role in that play—perhaps as a space pilot, the daddy, a superhero, or family baby. Emphasize your pride in a class where all help each other to enjoy play. Watch with wonder as other children in your group engage and interact in their play with a worried, compulsive, upset, or withdrawn child. Often, in the magic way that young children have, a peer can entice that isolated child into the story world to share a play theme. By including the worried child into their fantasy world, the other children help lighten that child's inner tensions as they engage him or her in the world of imaginative and healing classroom play.

ANSWER CHILDREN'S EMOTIONAL QUESTIONS HONESTLY AND BRIEFLY

Children feel anxious when they think adults have secrets that are scary. They often ask startling questions. After Livia's grandma died, she asked the teacher, "When will my daddy die?" Try to answer children's questions about death or destruction reassuringly. Remember that a young preschooler finds it hard to grasp the finality of death. In a television-rerun program, such as *Roadrunner*, preschoolers may have watched Coyote be run over by a steam shovel and have tar poured over him, and then he turns up quite alive and raring for a fight in the next episode.

If a child has been taken to a funeral service and anxiously asks next day in child care about whether the caregiver or his mom or dad will die, respond in a clear, comforting way. Furman (1974) has written that when a child asks a nurturing adult, "Can this happen to me or my mommy?" the answer should take into account the child's sense of time. An adult might be hesitant to say, "No, I won't die," or "Your mom or dad won't die," because we all do eventually die. Yet if a parent or caregiver says, "Yes, I will die," the child understands this to mean tomorrow or next week! Furman has recommended that the parent answer, "No, I do not expect to die for a long, long time," stressing the "no," and add that you expect to enjoy the child as a grown-up (p. 37).

LISTEN EMPATHETICALLY

After the tragedy of September 11, 2001, many preschoolers played out crashing scenes of airplanes bombing and crashing into their block towers in the classroom. Others not only played out their fears but also expressed them verbally. It relieves a young child when his beloved caregivers and parents affirm clearly that they are strong and will protect the child from any bad people who try to hurt him. Listen empathetically to a child's complaints, worries, fears, and hurt feelings. Your focused and respectful attention often relieves a child's stress.

CONCLUSIONS

There are many strategies that teachers can use to increase classroom peacefulness and reduce stress. Such strategies range from listening intently to children to encouraging fun activities such as dancing and playing to relieve tension. Many suggestions that were described in this chapter can be personalized as necessary and as the situation permits. As time passes and you deepen the children's trust in your genuine caring for them, they will accept an even greater array of signals and stories, activities and techniques that you create in order—in turn—to broaden and deepen the caring relationships among the children and between the children and yourself. Their essential feelings of security and surety in your nurturing and in your always being *for* them will give you the freedom to create even more ways in which to increase feelings of comfort and well being within each child.

STUDY QUESTIONS

Why is it important to teach children concepts of *same* and *different*?

How can you encourage and create conversations with children from diverse backgrounds?

What are some ways you can carry out tension-relieving exercises during circle time?

What are some activities that can be used to enhance children's self-esteem?

When is it important to slow down your pace during some transition times for children?

When is it important to quicken your pace for other transition times?

CHAPTER

USING STORYTELLING TO RELIEVE CHILD STRESSES

Storytelling fascinates children and adults. Cultivate a storytelling-mode voice, whether you are reading a tale, telling a made-up story just for a particular child, or even telling the children about when you were a child. Stories help folks forget their worries. The act of reading a story to a child about another child who was helped during a stressful and sad time is sometimes called "bibliotherapy." Stories that are considered bibliotherapy have positive resolutions; the goal of reading the story is to help the child who is listening to gain comfort and courage.

HONE YOUR ORAL STORYTELLING SKILLS

You have probably noticed that when young children are fussing while waiting for food or to go outdoors, you can decrease their distress when you go into storytelling mode. Tell a fascinating brief story at lunchtime when the children seem droopy and tired, perhaps because food delivery is delayed. While the children listen to you, they will become less stressed and more likely to eat better if they perk up to listen to your story. Five-year-old Carrie announced that she was not hungry while the other preschoolers started eating lunch. Using her special storytelling voice, Ms. Madeleine started telling a tale of long ago. Shari Lewis (1989) included a different version of this tale in her book of 1-minute stories.

> Once, long, long ago, the beautiful Queen of Sheba came on a trip, in a caravan of camels laden with precious gifts. She came on a visit to King Solomon because she had heard that he was the wisest man in the world. The King welcomed her with great courtesy, with many delicious banquets (with wonderful yummy foods), and with many entertainments. In return for King Solomon's hospitality, the queen spread before him a precious gift she had brought. The servants spread out on the floor a rug woven and embroidered beautifully with flowers. Then, smiling, the Queen invited the king to determine which one of the flowers among the hundreds on the carpet was a real flower, and not one of the hundreds of skillfully embroidered blossoms. How could the king solve this puzzle? As he looked over this magnificent gift, all the flowers seemed so exquisitely glowing with life-like gorgeous colors. The king casually asked one of his servants to open a window in the palace throne room, to let in some fresh air. Then, he studied the carpet very carefully. Soon, his eyes lit up and he pointed to a flower on the rug, and told the Queen that one was the real flower. The Queen of Sheba was amazed! She was really puzzled! How had the King figured out the answer to the clever question she has asked in order to find out how smart he was? When the window was opened, King Solomon quietly noticed that a tiny bee flew in the window on a breeze. And of course, the baby bee went straight for the real flower and ignored all the lovely flowers figured on the rug. Soon afterwards, the bee flitted out the window. The Queen had not seen the tiny insect that had helped the King solve the puzzle of which flower was real among all those beautiful fake flowers. The queen was convinced that indeed King Solomon was the wisest person in the world!

As the teacher slowly and dramatically told this tale, Carrie stopped fussing and started eating her food. She was entranced while listening and enjoying the mystery of King Solomon's clever guess.

PERSONALIZE STORIES TO PROVIDE POSITIVE SOLUTIONS TO EASE A SPECIFIC STRESS

Brett (1986), an Australian clinician, described beautifully the technique she used to help Amantha, her own child, when she was faced initially with the stress Amantha felt. The 3-year-old child knew that in a couple of weeks she would have to start to go to school. She confided, "Mommy, there's a headache in my tummy" (p. 1). Her child's plight galvanized Brett to create stories about a little girl, Annie, whose name and family situation (including parents and a dog) is similar to her own child's.

Teachers can adapt this Annie-story technique to create a tailormade story to deal with a specific stress for a specific child. The listening child identifies with the story character and is able to try what the character in the story has done to lessen a felt stress. For example, in your own Annie story, if a child loses friends because she always insists on her own way; let the character in your made-up story discover new and more positive ways to interact with other children. You can act out the new ways by playing Annie and asking the child to act as a classmate.

In one of the Annie Stories that Brett created, she related that Annie was able to imagine that she had a fairy godmother with magic powers. In one episode, the fairy godmother invites Annie to fly over the neighborhood with her. Annie has told her parents that she is scared to go to a birthday party at her friend's house. When she previously visited on a play date, that family's dog barked a lot and scared Annie. Yet Annie longs to go to the party. The fairy godmother helps Annie to imagine that her friend's little dog barks at the gate when Annie comes by to visit because he really wishes Annie would be friendly with him; the dog thinks she does not like him. Annie rethinks her problem with the dog in a new way.

In the Annie stories, an adult can suggest magic that will comfort and ease a child's worry or fear. When her child had nightmares, Brett created a different Annie story for her. In this story, Annie's mom gave her child a magic invisible ring and carefully put the pretend ring on Annie's finger before she went to bed. The mom told Annie that this ring had so much powerful magic that none of the monsters would be able to get to Annie in her dreams. This technique worked wonderfully for Amantha. Brett additionally suggested that you give a child crayons and encourage the child to draw his or her feelings about the stressful situation.

CREATE PLAYLETS OUT OF CHILDREN'S STORIES THAT THEY DICTATE TO YOU

Paley (1990) invented a technique to empower children to tell their own stories and then choose other children in the group to act out the characters' story roles. The teacher gives every child a chance to tell a story. Of course, some children's stories may be about television characters, superheroes, and monsters. The teacher accepts each child's story. Often stories embody absurd contradictions, such as a horrible wolf eating up kids, but then somehow the children all escape and get safely home to Mama. Paley described how she elicits and writes down each child's stories. She gives power to each child to choose the players for that small drama. Her technique attests to her deep respect as a teacher for the healing power of each child's individual storytelling efforts as a way to come to terms with their inner struggles.

USING STORYTELLING TO RELIEVE STRESS

Read special picture books that deal with *specific* troubles, worries, angers, and frustrations of young children in order to reassure and calm them. Many children's picture books address a specific topic of stress in a young child's life.

Choose Books that Deal with Stress

Choose a variety of picture books that deal with different themes of stress for a child. Books are available for young children that deal with scary and difficult situations, such as parental abandonment and/or death of a loved family member. *You Hold Me and I'll Hold You* is a comforting book about a young girl whose mom has left the family (Carson, 1992). Her dad has to drive with her to the funeral of his own sister. The little girl feels upset as she watches all the adults crying during the church service. She herself decides she can feel comfortable and okay if she settles on her daddy's lap and they hug each other.

Some picture books deal with illness, such as a beloved grandpa's debilitating stroke (dePaola, 1981). Other books deal with stresses that seem mild to a parent, such as when a family moves away from the neighborhood where the child's best friend lived.

In a series of Scholastic books, Metzger describes upset feelings of little dinosaurs, such as being afraid to start school or distress when peers announce, "I'm not your friend!", or the resentful feelings of the other dinosaurs in class if a little dinosaur announces "I'm the boss!" In one of these stories (Metzger, 1998), Tara, a little dinosaur, was afraid of the ocean when the children went to the beach. She did not feel brave enough to go in the water. Then Tara's teacher asked her to think of times when Tara *had* acted bravely. Tara remembered enjoying holding the lizard that the pet store owner had brought to school when the other kids did not want to touch it. Soon Tara began to smile, and was then willing to let the teacher hold her hand and walk her into the water to splash around with the other children.

Don't Touch describes the exasperation of a child who is told not to touch his Grandpa's fishing tackle, not to touch the cake his uncle has just baked, and on and on (Kline, 1985). In his own playroom, he pounds and shapes playdough until he is able to get out his frustrated feelings. Then he puts a sign on his playroom door that says, "Keep out!" This boy copes with his frustrating experiences of being given negative orders by putting just such a negative order for others on his own door!

Choose Books that Are Proactively Useful

Some books are *proactively* useful. When you choose to read these books, you are encouraging child empathy, consideration, kindness, and helpfulness in future interactions. Your book-reading choices increase the chances that children will learn more optimal ways to think about, deal with, and decrease any future stresses. British books by Nick Butterworth (1996) feature Percy, the groundskeeper in the park. Percy kindly and cheerfully helps out the small animals in distress in his park. Hedgehog is crying because his sharp spines inevitably result in his bursting any balloon he is given at a birthday party. Percy devises a clever solution. Taking his box of corks, he carefully caps each sharp spine with a cork. Now Hedgehog happily holds a balloon at a birthday party, and it bobs up and down in the breeze safely without popping.

In *Dogger*, another British tale, Dave, the baby of the family, cannot go to sleep without his old Dogger to snuggle with (Hughes, 1989). One day, his mom wheels him in his stroller to the schoolyard to pick up his big sister Bella from school; somehow he loses his toy dog. His folks look everywhere at bedtime but cannot find his old beloved snuggly doggie. Very upset, he cannot get to sleep. But next day, by accident, Dogger, found on the pavement of the schoolyard, is put up for sale with other toys at the school fair. Dave's big sister spies the girl who purchased the toy doggie for a few pennies at the toy table. Despite Bella's pleading, that girl will not give back Dave's animal toy. Then Bella decides to do something very generous and kind. She has just won a fancy plush bear at the fair. In order to get back Dogger for her little brother, Bella trades her plush bear to the girl in exchange for Dogger. Bella gives Dogger to her baby brother, and Dave can relax and feel happy again.

Dr. Seuss's books showcase Horton the elephant in delightful rhymes and illustrations. Horton is faithful one hundred percent in the book *Horton Hatches an Egg* (Seuss, 1954). Horton agrees to babysit for her egg while the mother bird takes a brief vacation. But she stays away for months! Through miserable weather and lonesome times, Horton keeps his word and keeps taking care of the egg.

Horton is a true friend to the tiny beings living on a flower petal in *Horton Hears a Who* (Seuss, 1956), even when monkeys and other animals ridicule him for his persistence in trying to save the tiny creatures whose cries for help only Horton is sensitive enough to hear. Bill Cosby's book, *Little Bill: The Meanest Thing to Say* (1997), provides children with a word to say ("So?") when a bully tries to enlist the kids to say more and more mean things about each other.

Choose stories to give a boost in self-esteem to little children who feel small and sometimes helpless in the world of big grown-ups and older siblings. Six year-old Roy loved to hear Dr. Seuss's book, *The King's Stilts* (1955). In this story, a courageous little pageboy to the king at the palace decides to dig up the king's stilts. A nasty vizier at court had stolen and then buried the stilts. The king was so sad. He had always rejoiced as he went off later each afternoon with his page as both played on stilts. Going about on stilts was the king's way to play and unwind at the end of a busy, working royal day. The message, that a little boy could feel scared and yet act courageous, resonated with Roy. He asked to hear that story almost every day for a few weeks.

The picture book story *The Little Engine that Could* fascinates young children (Piper, 1997). The big engine refuses to help bring toys over the mountain to boys and girls. But the little engine does not want the children to be disappointed. Small as she is, she huffs and puffs and tries hard to pull the train over the mountain while carrying toys for the children's sakes. Once, while Miss Madeleine was reading this story to several children, one 5-year-old, listening intently, sucked dreamily on his thumb. As she read, he briefly took his thumb out of his mouth and nodded approvingly about the little engine in a whisper, "That was very nice of her. That was *very* nice of her!"

Hiawatha's Kind Heart (Walt Disney Productions, 1986) is the story of a young American Indian boy who sets out to paddle his canoe to an island. The boy wants to prove that he can hunt with his bow and arrow just the way the brave men in his tribe hunt. But his kind heart causes him, instead, to rescue and protect animals he sees, such as a baby squirrel, a mama partridge, and a young deer. While Hiawatha is eating some tasty berries from a bush, a big grouchy bear decides that it is *his* bush. The big grouchy bear chases Hiawatha. All the animals Hiawatha had spared earlier then pitch in to help Hiawatha run away safely and get back to his canoe. Squirrels throw nuts down at the angry bear; a beaver gnaws down a log to trip up the bear.

For kindergarten-age children, Grahame's (1983) book *The Reluctant Dragon* puts an entirely different spin on the story of St. George and the dragon. The dragon writes poetry and is befriended by a young boy, who is calm, sensible, and has good ideas to solve problems. The villagers call on St. George to come to their village, go up on their mountain, and kill the dragon. The boy arranges for his friend the dragon and St. George to carry out a mock fight so that it will seem that St. George wins. But neither the dragon nor the knight is hurt. At the end, all march down to the village for a big victory feast.

Choose Books that Address Children's Struggles with Bad Feelings

Some books address young children's struggles with bad feelings when excluded from play with older siblings and friends. *Jamaica Tag-Along* tells the story of Jamaica, a young African American girl whose big brother excludes her from his play with friends (Havill, 1989). Later, Jamaica is building a castle in the sand box. She finds herself using the same words to keep away a younger child who asks to play with her in the sandbox. Jamaica suddenly realizes that the younger boy feels as sad as she did. So then she invites the little boy to play. When big brother finishes playing ball with his friends, he comes over and is excited to see Jamaica's sand towers. When her brother asks if he can participate in the sand building, Jamaica smiles. She cheerfully invites him to come and join them.

In Hoban's (1994) picture book *Best Friends for Frances,* the badger, Frances, addresses this same problem. She feels resentful and upset at being excluded from play. This story ends with the same kind of positive decision. After first deciding to retaliate for being excluded, Frances later decides that all the animals playing and having a picnic together is more fun for everyone.

Picture books often admirably focus on the specific resentments, angers, and worries a child may feel. Using Black English dialect, Clifton's (1975) warmly engaging story, *My Brother Fine with Me,* describes the harassed and frustrated feelings of a sister who must watch her little brother every day of the summer while her parents are at work. She tells herself that she is glad when he announces to her that he is going to run away from home. She even helps him pack. Then, reminiscing by herself, she starts to remember good things about little brother. How relieved big sister is on opening the front door to find him sitting right there on the front steps! Running away is not easy for a preschooler.

Children's ability to find another nurturing adult in the family, when upset by a parent's demands or decisions, is beautifully reflected in *Something from Nothing* (Gilman, 1992). In this lovingly illustrated tale set in a shtetl (a Jewish prewar village in Europe), Grandpa sewed Joseph a blanket when the boy was born. As he outgrows his blanket, Joseph's mama exclaims that it is time to throw it out. With stout confidence in his Grandpa, the tailor, the little boy each time exclaims that his grandpa can fix it and runs down the street to his grandpa for help. Indeed, his kindly grandpa over the years transforms the material still left into a coat, a jacket, a vest, a handkerchief, and finally the covering for a button. Then the button is lost! But the little boy triumphantly finds comfort in his own creative idea: there is just enough "material" in this saga to create a story to share with his schoolmates. Children love the cadences of this story, the kindliness, the feeling that special family members understand a child's upset feelings and will work wonders to help the loved child.

Discuss Children's Own Feelings About Familiar Classic Stories Reflecting Stress for the Characters

Children are generally quite familiar with the retelling of classic stories, even if only in the television version. Ask each of the children how they would have acted. How do they feel about the troubles in a story with a scary situation, such as *The Three Billy Goats Gruff, Goldilocks and the Three Bears,* or *The Three Little Pigs?* One preschooler suggested, "Goldilocks should write a letter to Baby Bear saying how sorry she was." Another child said Goldilocks should invite the bear family to her house for cookies and milk. As children talk about how scary certain stories are and offer their own reflections on the "scary parts," teachers gain insights into the children's own fears.

Some stories that enchant children still have parts that are too painful for them to watch or hear about. The wicked witch in *The Wonderful Wizard of Oz* (Baum, 2000/1900) and the Lion Aslan in *The Chronicles of Narnia* (Lewis, 1994/1956) are both characters that some preschoolers have told a teacher not to talk about or show them. How can you help those children feel safe when the others do want to hear these stories? If a child tells you that a story was too scary when her family tried to read it with her, then perhaps you can let that child choose to play safely (within your visual range) at a different activity while you read the story with the rest of the children. Alternate activities could include a clay table, doll corner, small blocks, or puzzles. Giving choices will help the child feel empowered, and also feel more comfortable at not being required to sit when the child is feeling worried about a story he or she thinks will be "scary." Just as we are considerate about children's different preferences for clothes or foods, we can be considerate about their preferences for stories.

Some books provide alternate endings to a child dilemma. The children are enabled to figure out how *they* would have solved the stressful situation. Crary has created a series of such books. *Willy's Noisy Sister* (2001) tells the story of a child annoyed by his little sister. Crary provides alternative responses, so that children listening to the story can decide what the brother should do to solve his stressful situation.

Read Poetry

Poetry has awesome powers to soothe the soul. Poetry has the power to express vividly the worries, hopes, and feelings of little children. From Robert Louis Stevenson's collection, *A Child's Garden of Verses* (1924), here is his quaint poem called *My Bed is a Little Boat* that expresses how comforting it is for little ones to be helped by routines, imaginary scenarios, and expressions of their wishes when it is bedtime:

My bed is like a little boat:
Nurse helps me in when I embark;
She girds me in my sailor's coat and starts me in the dark.

At night I go on board and say
Good-night to all my friends on shore:
I shut my eyes and sail away and see and hear no more.
And sometimes things to bed I take,
As prudent sailors have to do;
Perhaps a slice of wedding-cake,
Perhaps a toy or two.
All night across the dark we steer;
But when the day returns at last;
Safe in my room, beside the pier,
I find my vessel fast.

Another of his poems honestly expresses a child's need, even in the olden days, to play with his own stuff free of other children's interference:

When I am grown to man's estate
I shall be very proud and great;
And tell the other girls and boys
Not to meddle with my toys!

Poetry brings grins of delight that can settle restless children on a mat to listen to the riotous rhymes, such as those in the *Sheriff of Rottenshot* (Prelutsky, 1982). Each of these poems sets up a ridiculous situation, such as the plight of a lady kangaroo whose belongings were always falling out of her pouch; finally, a tailor solved her problem by putting in a neat zipper for her pouch! Prelutsky's zany humor includes a poem about a character who eats only the peels of bananas, rather than the bananas, and the wrappers from candy bars rather than the chocolate candy within!

CONCLUSIONS

Armed with dozens of possible ideas of ways to use storytelling to help stressed children, teachers and other child care providers feel more empowered. Storytelling inspires adult insights that allow us to individualize our choices of ways to cope with children's difficulties. You can find a bibliography of the children's books mentioned at the end of the book. These resources are often a powerful inspiration for children to aspire to learn and to try more coping skills to handle stresses they encounter in daily life.

STUDY QUESTIONS

Why is it important to hone your oral storytelling skills?

How can you personalize stories to ease stress for children?

What are some ways you can use storytelling to ease stress for children?

Why should you include poetry books when telling stories to children?

ADULT STRESS BUSTERS IN CARE SETTINGS AND SCHOOLS

WORKING WITH PARENTS, PERSONNEL, HOME VISITORS, SUPERVISORS, MENTAL HEALTH PROFESSIONALS, AND CONSULTANTS

Adults who work daily with children need ingenuity in handling stresses from combining this special work, which entails so many interpersonal and intellectual demands, with demands in their own family life. Caring for infants, toddlers, and young children is hard work, physically and emotionally. How can caregivers reduce stresses they are bound to feel from time to time? Adults can be amazingly creative in finding ways to handle stress positively. Some meditate. Some take up yoga. Some go for an early morning swim or a long run before breakfast. Some get their hair done; they feel better if they think they look better.

Most adults find that massage calms stress. Making love with a cherished, supportive spouse lowers stress. Vigorous work such as chopping wood for the fireplace unwinds some folks. Some go out and play poker all night for small stakes, cheering up after an evening with close companions. Counselors for senior citizens emphasize that close friends are a bulwark against stress and worrisome outcomes of growing older, such as depression.

What can we say about handling adult stresses in child care? Personnel troubles may occur. Some stresses arise in meetings or interactions with family members. Some stresses arise because a present stress on the job is dredging up unpleasant echoes of past personal stresses.

HANDLING STRESSES FROM PERSONNEL

Sometimes troubles happen between two staff members. Suppose a new staff member comes in and acts as if she knows the latest ways to redesign a classroom or to teach a specific lesson. Co-workers who have been there longer may feel indignant and psychologically muscled aside. Or a new staff member may feel that the other teachers are all old friends. They seem to stop a conversation abruptly if they are together on the playground and she walks over toward them. Relax. We all need time to get used to new co-workers. Try putting on a "temporary mask." *Act* more laid back until comfort sets in and you are now easily accepted as one of the crew of care providers.

Suppose that a particular adult who works at your facility is making unkind comments or telling others untrue tales about you that are then repeated to you. Be sure to write down, date, and describe each episode. You need to keep a paper trail describing each incident before you bring your case to your employer. Make sure to read the staff members' handbook to ensure that you are following protocol in going to the appropriate person designated to address your complaint.

Sometimes a new director finds that staff is unfriendly at first. Staff members were used to the former director. They may even wonder whether this new person took the job away from the former director. This is an example of *projection of evil,* since the change of directors was due to the former director's taking a new job, and the new director was not at all involved in that choice. Time and patience will usually work best to help staff feel comfortable with a new person in charge. As others see the cheerful, consistent, professional ways in which the new person is working and collaborating in the classroom, staff members will feel more and more accepting and welcoming.

HANDLING STRESSES FROM PARENTS

Sometimes staff stress comes from a parent's unfair accusations of a caregiver (Gillespie, 2006):

> Judith knew today would be a hard day. Jason is 20 months old and has bitten 3 children in the last week. Today Judith will meet with his parents. When they arrive, Judith greets them, offers something to drink, and asks about their day. She starts the meetings by saying, "Jason has been biting quite a bit lately, and we need to figure out what we can do to help him stop." Immediately Jason's father reacts: "Well, he doesn't ever bite at home, so something must be wrong here!" Judith is taken aback and doesn't know how to respond. (p. 53)

Techniques to Reduce Stress When Dealing With Parents

What techniques can you apply personally to bring down feelings of anger, worry, rage, or urges to get back at someone?

Active Listening: Your Most Powerful Tool!

If your concern is about something a parent says that is critical of you or denigrates or accuses the child, then try AL, the *Active Listening* technique pioneered by Gordon (1970, 2000). Pledge yourself to understand how upset that parent is. The parent may feel guilty leaving a baby in the care of unfamiliar people. Dad may feel angry and guilty that the baby seems to want to stay in your arms at pick-up time and not leap in his father's arms to go home. Think of the parent's worries rather than the criticisms and accusations.

Act Nurturing Toward a Complaining Parent

Suppose a mother who leaves her child in your family child care complains about something each day to you. Try nurturing the mom. Express admiration of the courage it takes to realize that the family needs a mother's second income from work outside the home as well as her mothering work. Express support for parental stress and how brave she is in trying so hard to handle both jobs.

Learn Developmental Norms
So You Can Reassure Nervous Parents

Some parents are so anxious that their child should be doing just what other children are doing at exactly the same age. They feel stressed if their child seems to be slower in sleeping through the night, potty learning, talking, or tying shoelaces. If a parent is worried about a child's behaviors and confides her frustration to you, listen and reflect the parent's underlying message.

A parent may worry that the child is not walking as early as others in the same age group. When you know developmental norms well, you can share information to calm a parent. Reassure the parent that walking, like getting teeth, is genetically programmed. Given opportunities to crawl about and pull up on sturdy furniture, children learn to walk within a *wide window* of time—anywhere from 6 to 18 months, normally. If a preschooler is having trouble with handling scissors, ask how many opportunities that child has to practice small-muscle skills at home. It may turn out that parents do not know about safety scissors for tots; up to now, they have forbidden the child ever to touch a pair of scissors. Assist the parents to feel comfortable to purchase a pair of safety scissors. At home they can then encourage their child to enjoy sculpting old newspaper pages into interesting cut shapes. The parent feels relieved that the child is just fine now that she has opportunities for safe practice. Try to find out, for each anxious stress a parent reveals, whether the child has had opportunities to learn the skill that the parent is concerned about.

During a home visit when Mom was away, and Grandma looked worried because her grandbaby at 11 months did not enter into a Pat-a-cake game with me as I cheerfully sang the song and tried to get him to clap hands together. She demanded to know if something was wrong. I explained that perhaps this was not a game he was familiar with. Sure enough, when she asked her daughter later on, the mom said that she had never tried that game with her little son. Once the adults started playing Pat-a-cake with their baby, he enthusiastically entered into the game. Always ask a parent about whether a young child has had an opportunity to learn the skill or information that the parent is worried about.

Wonder Together with Parents

If the parents are worried about a problem you have dealt with in the classroom and have asked for a meeting, try wondering aloud together with the parents. Ask gentle questions to find out more about how the parents feel. How do they see the situation? What are their ideas? Ask parents to work *with* you so that you all can try to understand what is causing the problem, such as biting, and how best to alleviate the distress. A toddler has little language to express frustrations. Maybe that child uses biting to express frustrations. In another case, a center classroom may be overstimulating, and a particular child might be less stressed if placed in a child care setting with fewer children per adult. *Wondering together* helps both caregiver and parents gain insights as to the tensions or stresses that are causing a child's difficult behaviors in the group. Wondering together helps both caregivers and parents think of plans to help the child feel less stress. Sometimes an earlier bedtime with less television may be a simple solution. Sometimes searching for a solution will take longer efforts by the concerned adults.

Help Parents Find Positive Attributes About Their Child

Suppose you are worried because a parent talks disparagingly to you about a child. Once at a parent group meeting, I asked parents in two different go-rounds to tell me something that upset them about their child. On the next round, they were to relate something they liked a lot about their child. Every mom expressed some strong upset or anger at a certain behavior of her preschooler. But a few moms could not think of one admired or happy aspect of their preschoolers to share with the group. Be alert when a parent expresses only negative feelings about a child. That parent is revealing a lot of adult stress. You might want to empathize that bringing up little children sure has some exasperating times. Then add a personal anecdote about that child; mention something delightful, kind, or creative you have really appreciated as a teacher.

If a parent talks down to you about the child, you could say reassuringly and kindly, "It sure does take a lot of patience and good humor to raise kids." Sometimes we really need to keep our cool and remember that kids will be kids. Children sometimes behave in ways we get annoyed about, but thank goodness we are the grown-ups. We love them no matter what, but sometimes we sure do need to pray for more patience!

Gently Explain Your Point of View When Working with Parents

What if a parent gives you orders as a care provider that you feel are developmentally inappropriate for a child? A parent might complain that she wants you to prevent her toddler from napping so that she can put him to bed earlier at home. Gently describe how sleepy and tired the toddler is after lunch. Share with the parent how refreshed and raring to go he feels after his nap and what a delightful little fellow he is then when playing with his friends.

What if a parent demands that you have his child out of diapers in a few weeks, or he will yank the child from your care? Agree how wonderful it feels when a child has learned to go potty. Explain that teachers look for signs of a child's *readiness* for toilet learning. Share some of these child signs with the parent: Can the toddlers say *poop* and *pee?* Is she able to sit still for a few minutes? Is he alert to his own body signals when about to poop (Honig, 1993)? Work *with* the parent. You are both going to watch for and encourage these early signs of readiness. Then, when you both are clear that the prerequisites are in place, the child will indeed be ready for potty learning.

Listen to a Parent's Ideas

For some stresses, you may well need to enlist a *parent's good ideas* to help you cope with a child stress. A parent may suggest an easing of tensions when leaving in the morning by asking the caregiver to establish a special routine. The adult might want to bring the child in arms to the window so the tot can watch the parent wave and blow an extra kiss from outside the building before going off to work. Some problems are more easily solved in cooperation with families. Transitions to child care for infants and toddlers involve stressful feelings of separation. Be patient. Enlist ideas from family members, including grandparents, on ways to ease the stress of separation and transition into group care (Xu, 2006).

Help Parents Learn How to
Play One-to-One with Their Child

Some child care facilities are fortunate to have a social worker or outreach parent worker on staff. When you notice that a particular child comes into care with gloomy or tense reactions after weeks in the program, you will want to ask for support from the outreach staff. Their work can be so positive in reducing child stress. Researchers (Dickinson, 2006) working with poor families in the Caribbean assigned children 9–24 months to receive a milk supplement, weekly stimulating play sessions with their mom, both conditions, or none. When the children grew to late adolescence, their mental health functioning was assessed. The psychosocial assessments revealed less anxiety, depression, and antisocial behavior among the youths whose *mothers had been taught to play with them individually* when they were younger than 5 years.

Outreach workers had taught the mothers how to play individually with a young child. Mothers then paid attention to signs of fatigue or to protests that signaled a child was upset with too-vigorous play. They looked for a child's expressions of real pleasure in the playful interaction. Encouraging parents to do more child watching increases their genuine interest in their child's development. These *noticing skills* become wonderful catalysts for decreasing stress in their children's lives, even when families are living in difficult circumstances.

Remember Your Goal Is to Help the Child

Despite the best efforts of intervention programs, some parental stress is so high that programs cannot provide comfort and supports for parents. Even trained outreach staff may not be able to reduce stress and worry as much as they wish. An intervention program in Turkey succeeded in decreasing depression, but not stress, in parents of children with disabilities (Kucuker, 2006). Remember that your main goal is to enhance young children's lives. Supporting change for more optimal family patterns is a challenge even for agencies and personnel specializing in this work.

HANDLING STRESSES INVOLVING SEXUALITY ISSUES

Personal hang-ups of adults in the domain of sexuality can add to child distress. Some children snuggle down on their cots at naptime and gently stroke their genitals to soothe themselves into sleep. Some adults do not feel comfortable that children have sensual needs (Honig, 2000). Even though the lights are dim and the child is under covers, the adult may feel tense and critical.

Address Any Personal Shame About Private Body Parts and Children's Sensuality

One teacher proudly reported to me that she made the toddlers sleep with their hands outside the coverlet so that they would not touch themselves "down there." Her remarks revealed her own unexamined strong discomfort with sexual parts or masturbation. Caregivers need to face honestly their own hang-ups about children's sensual or sexual behaviors.

Adults need to separate normative child behaviors from more compulsive behaviors that truly indicate worrisome child stresses.

Accept that Normal Youngsters Do Have Curiosity About Bodies

Young kids are endlessly fascinated with each other's bodies. They are amazed that another toddler has a belly button. They are very comfortable at peeing together while sitting on potties. In a French crèche for infants and toddlers, I once watched 20 toddlers sitting companionably together on their potties at the same time in a room. Little children do not have adult hang-ups or shame about body parts. Indeed, the toddler daughter of one psychiatrist confided to her papa who was tucking her in at night that "this is my best feeling part" as she patted her vulva. Work on strong tensions you may have about children's exploratory curiosities. Of course, you cannot let children invade each other's body parts. Those are private spaces. Choose easy-to-understand and gentle books that explain sexual differences and possible worries in simple terms for young children to understand (Gordon & Gordon, 1974a, 1974b).

As adults we may find it a challenge to work hard to get rid of stresses associated with adult feelings of shame about bodies. Erikson's work (1950) as a child psychologist revealed how devastating shame can be for shriveling children's feelings about their bodies and themselves. Shame corrodes a child's soul! Little kids do stuff that adults may blush at or even be shocked at. A preschooler once proudly informed me that he had eaten the "boogie" he picked out of his nose.

Teachers should be ready with interest and a calmer readiness to learn more from child watching about the fascinating ways young children reason and the interesting repertoire of behaviors that very young children can exhibit. Adults can even enjoy being occasionally startled and amused! A toddler wants to scratch an itch under his scrotum and reaches into his pants to do so casually for just a moment. A little girl has an itch on her tummy and lifts her dress way above her panties to get at the itchy place. Teachers need to create innovative ways to calm their own stress when faced with unexpected child behaviors that involve body nether regions!

A graduate student came to talk to me about her research work. She brought her 3-year-old with her and asked Daisy, the secretary downstairs, to please watch the little one. Both had often been visitors to the building, and the child was familiar with Daisy. A while later Daisy rushed upstairs and knocked on my office door. She looked white as a ghost and agitatedly asked me to come outside my office. She was almost trembling. It seems the little girl had taken down her pants and was proudly sticking her bottom out, spreading the cheeks, and somewhat doubled over, parading about the reception room downstairs. I popped my head into my office and calmly told the student that I would be back in a minute and closed the door. Then I went downstairs, greeted the little girl, and matter-of-factly remarked, "Well, honey, you sure have shown us your tush and the hole where you make a poop. You have shown them to Ms. Daisy for quite a while. Now it is time to pull up your panties. And I will find some paper and crayons for you to draw us a picture." Satisfied with the definite acknowledgement that she had indeed shown off her body parts quite thoroughly, she pulled up her pants, accepted some paper and crayons, and sat down to draw a picture to show us when I would be finished talking with her mommy.

Identify Troubling Sexualized Behaviors

Are there times when sexualized behaviors should be a worry for a teacher? Yes! Compulsive sexual behaviors are a sign of child stress and perhaps even of abuse. If you are worried about a child who masturbates compulsively during the day rather than at naptime, or seems to have adult knowledge about sexuality, be sure to consult with your director. Read articles and books on how to handle occasions when a child reveals that she or he may have been molested and sworn to secrecy (Wachter, 1983).

How should you note troubling signs of body abuse? If you are diapering a baby and see quite worrisome bruises or signs of intrusion at the vulva or anus, be sure to write down and describe what you have observed and date your description. Then ask your director to read your note. Together you can find ways to decrease your stress by keeping up further observations or by deciding with your supervisor that this observation absolutely requires calling a hotline. Teachers are designated reporters of child abuse. All teachers are required reporters—whether for suspicions of sexual abuse or to report that a child's back shows stripe marks from a whip or cigarette burns on buttocks or hands.

HANDLING STRESSES FOR HOME VISITORS

In some programs, all caregivers are also required to make a certain number of home visits. In other programs, home visitors form a separate cadre of service providers for the program. Not all neighborhoods are safe places for home visitors. Yet these providers are gifted at forming and maintaining supportive contacts with families in order to enhance chances for children to flourish in the home as well as center or school settings. Home visitors experience stresses similar to and yet often different from in-center staff.

A home visitor from the Family Development Research Program (Lally, Mangione, & Honig, 1988) confided during an in-service weekly meeting how nervous she had felt during one visit that week. When she knocked on the door of a mother's apartment to keep an appointment at a time that the mother had asked for, the mother was not there. A strange man opened the door, grinned, and locked the door behind her. The home visitor did some quick thinking. She explained about visiting the mother and toddler and asked for information on where the mom was. At first he refused information and refused to unlock the door. The situation was defused when she offered to bring him some beer and he told her the address where the mother could be found.

Schedule In-Service Role-Playing of Potentially Stressful Episodes

Role-playing and sharing experiences together with a supervisor are often helpful in decreasing the stresses of the home worker. A home visitor came to the door of one of the families in her caseload. The television was turned on high volume. Grandmother stood barring the doorway and said that the mom was out. Role-playing practice during intensive in-service training sessions really helped in this case. The home visitor was prepared with her response. She showed her credentials. She calmly assured the grandmother that the mother herself had made the appointment for this hour. Then she asked politely whether she could please sit and wait for Mom to return, which happened soon after.

Another home visitor was becoming stressed during each visit because every seat in the apartment was cluttered with soiled diapers or other messy material. On the next visit, she rang the doorbell and asked the mother earnestly for some old newspapers so that she could leave her drippy messy boots, full of snow and spring mud, outside the apartment door. She thanked the mom gratefully for bringing her the old newspapers so that she did not have to "mess up" the mother's apartment with her drippy boots. This marvelously creative action had amazing results. During the next few home visits, the mom had obviously made an attempt to clean up some of her living space. Expressing concern and gratitude for others often releases their ability to give back a courtesy. This technique can work even when the other person is unaware that as a professional you have set up a *kindness-exchange scenario.* One home visitor helped the mom wash, dry, and put away a pile of dirty dishes she noticed in the sink before she settled down with Mom for the home visit whose goal that day was to provide mom with ideas to cope with her child's tantrums at bedtime. Finding a way to relate so that the child or adult who is stressed feels we are being extra understanding and kind will most likely help that person calm down and feel better. This calm attitude will allow the relationship interactions to go forward rather than be stuck in suspicious, hostile, or defensive modes.

Role-playing during in-service training times is a creative way to anticipate problems and wrestle with possible ways to handle them before a stressful event might happen. Such role-playing facilitates *positive-solution thinking* by a home visitor who feels tense when a parent comments critically on his or her plans with the child during a home visit.

Use Storytelling Techniques

Ms. Honey was visiting a single mom with a 13-month-old child. She had brought a Curious George book with her. After talking a while with Mom, the home visitor settled on the floor with the book, and the baby snuggled close to her. The mom looked at the book and remarked sharply that she hid all the books in a chest because her little girl tore books and was not ready for books at all. The home visitor turned to look gently and kindly at the mom. "It will be all right," she reassured the mom in a soothing voice. Then she proceeded to read the book at a level appropriate for the baby. "Look at the nice monkey! Pretty monkey. See his tail? Here's his tail. He has lots of brown fur. Feel his brown fur all over him. And he has two bright eyes. Can you point to his eye? Good for you. And where is his other eye? Yes. There is his other eye. You found it!" After spending lots of time on that page, the home visitor hooked her finger into the next page and asked the baby to turn the page for her. "Good page turning," she then praised the child. "Oh, look what's on this page. Another monkey! Hi, nice monkey. Can you find his long furry tail, lovey?" The book reading went on for quite a while as the little girl in delighted surprise found and pointed to another monkey on each page.

This technique of book reading respects the baby's level of ability. The adult *adapts the story* to captivate and enchant a child. The adult's picture-book sharing technique (Honig, 2003a) convinces a parent that indeed the child can attend to and enjoy books at an early age. Teachers of infants and toddlers need to think of themselves as being in charge of a story. With very young children, read with a theatrical flair. Feel free to change the story. To interest and captivate a baby who looks cranky and squirms away when the story is read as written, try to simplify. Add special words and use engaging voice tones rather than sticking to the exact text. After the home visit described above, the mom went to a local library and began taking out lots of books, with the advice and help of the children's librarian. Instead of tearing books or ignoring them, her little girl began to relish book-sharing times with mom. Their new special book-sharing time together increased the mother's confidence and the young toddler's experience of loving interactions with mom.

Choose Highly Interesting Books for Children

What other ideas will reduce worry in a disappointed parent who confides to you that her young child seems uninterested in books? How can you help a school-age child and the family who worry that the child has dyslexia—troubles learning to decode letters, meanings, or text? From interviews with successful adults who had severe difficulties in childhood, research shows that choosing books with materials of high interest and topics of special attractiveness to the individual child galvanizes the struggling reader to try hard (Fink, 2006). The child may still have difficulties with reading other materials. Choose books with topics of passionate interest so that a child with dyslexia is more likely to be successful when attempting to read. Your special efforts will lessen discouragement and enhance the child's self-esteem. Tutoring helps. Research has shown that some children lag in hearing language sounds. Children have troubles blending sounds, as in the word *street,* which is difficult for some preschoolers to pronounce. In learning to read, some children confuse the letters *b* with *d* or *p* with *q*. The earlier that adults recognize and seek help for language troubles, the less the chance of reading difficulties when the child reaches elementary school. This is not only an intellectual challenge for a child. Children who have difficulty pronouncing words may be neglected and even rejected by preschool playmates. Children who have difficulty learning to read when they reach school age feel frustration and decreased self-esteem.

Realize that Children Carry Emotional Stresses

Stress-busting requires that we consider with ingenuity *all* the ways that we can enhance children's readiness for early learning as a way to ensure their emotional and social well-being as well as cognitive competence.

HANDLING STRESSES BY WORKING WITH SUPERVISORS, MENTAL HEALTH PROFESSIONALS, AND CONSULTANTS

The severity of some children's stresses will require teachers to enlist mental health professionals more proactively. When keen and thorough observations have convinced a teacher that a child's stress is more serious than continuous nurturing classroom care can alleviate, then a teacher's first action should be to consult with administrators and supervisors. Supervisors often have knowledge of community resources that are available for helping. Some clinical programs at universities are eager to partner with child care and school facilities. These university programs need to place their graduate students in internships (often requiring up to 500 hours of clinical services) so that the clinicians-in-training can practice and deepen the clinical skills they are learning in the classroom. Such services are particularly helpful when a child care facility does not have extra funding for mental health services nor access to professionals who charge fees.

Sometimes a school can partner informally with a nearby hospital so that young residents who have had psychiatric training can come to advise teachers or to work with families and children experiencing troubling stresses.

Decide When You Need to Seek Professional Supports

Situations that involve horrible losses or trauma for a child who is in our care impel us to search for professional help. In particular, a teacher may want to seek out special support for a grieving child whose parent has cancer or if a child loved by the others in the classroom is injured in a terrible auto accident. But enlisting professionals to understand puzzling behaviors may help in other situations too. In one center, a little girl got on top of a boy in a closet, pretending to "hump him," as the upset and puzzled teachers reported. The visiting consultant made inquiries and found out that the little girl's grandpa had died several weeks before. Nobody, not even the mom, had told the teachers. The child was using simulated sexualized actions that revealed her upset feelings to the staff. Grandpa had been the only adult male figure in her life. Working with a psychologist, who was called in for a consultation, the teachers gained more insight into the nonsexual and sorrowful loss that was the basis for this child's acting-out behaviors.

This new knowledge galvanized the teachers to choose appropriate *bibliotherapy* books to read about the death of a grandparent or the death of a beloved pet. The teachers also talked with the children in the class about how sad children feel if a grandparent dies. The teachers enlisted the other children to think of ways they could be comforting with their classmate; the little girl had loved her grandpa so much and was feeling sad after her grandpa died.

Enlist Other Professionals within the School

In some cases, outside help may not be needed. Schools often have a school psychologist or counselor who is well trained to provide special supports for a troubled child. When bitter divorce fights are affecting a student's grades as well as increasing aggressive behaviors on the playground, a teacher can turn for supports to a widely offered school program that is called *Banana Splits*. This program is staffed by a social worker or other mental health specialist in the school. This specialist meets with groups of children stressed by family separation or divorce and custody battles. The children share their stories and their feelings. The adult leader helps the children understand that they did not cause the marital breakup. The leader also helps children find ways to share distress with each other and ways to heal from their hurt and sorrow. Many community agencies have resources that aid adults in supporting the difficult struggle of a young child to understand and cope with anguish at parental fighting and separation (Marquardt, 2005).

Set Up Liaisons Between Parents and Other Professionals

Sometimes parents express strong worries about a child's emotional difficulties or language development. They want extra specialized help for the child beyond the excellent nurturing care the teachers are providing. In one center, parents confided that they were very worried that their child's articulation problems were interfering with his ability to make friends. He was particularly shy and, in addition, his peers could not understand him. At the family's request and offer to pay extra for a specialist, the director contacted a psychologist specializing in language as well as in social skills with children. The director generously offered the specialist the opportunity to come and observe the child at free-play times in the center. Thinking creatively, the director even provided a small private space in the center where the specialist could bring the child and work with him individually. The parents were relieved and glad to pay for this extra service. The child was able to stay right in the center and was able to practice new skills with his peers. The director's generosity, positive invitation, and respect for other professionals resulted in the center becoming known as a place that not only provided quality care for young children but was very willing to allow professionals in to observe and then work on site with a child in special situations.

Arrange for Outside Help if a Child's Stress Results from a Family Loss

Sometimes finding outside professional help is urgently necessary. The gravest loss and stress for a young child occurs with the death of a loved parent. If this deep sorrow happens to a child in your care, inquire if there are special community programs for children who are grieving. Hospice organizations help. In Liverpool, New York, the Center for Living with Loss, together with Hospice, offer after-school programs for children suffering this stress. For a few summer days they provide a camp experience called Camp Healing Hearts (Haus, 2006). Daily for the first hour of camp, the children participate in a Healing Circle. Each day the circle focuses the children on different goals, such as tell your story, try to know your feelings, and decide what to do with your feelings. The final sessions focus on coping skills and talk about hope.

Ask for Help When a Child Has Disabilities that Require Extra Professional Skills

In an inclusive classroom, when you have a child who needs extra help, such as catheterization or occupational therapy sessions, reach out to organizations that can assist you to teach all the children, despite the particular troubles some may have. When services are provided, a teacher's stress level lowers and the teacher becomes more firmly committed to helping all the children flourish. Otherwise inclusion may be in name only. In one classroom, a toddler with hydrocephaly lay in his crib for hours. He could not lift his large head. The teacher and the other toddlers animatedly carried out an interesting activity at a nearby table. The toddler with a severe disability was not included. The teacher might have used a slant board to strap that child near the table so that he would have been able to see the children at their playful work. Professional helpers can often introduce equipment and ideas that will affirm a teacher's commitment to creating an inclusive classroom.

Keep a List of Consultants for a Variety of Different Emergencies

Every director needs to have a list of professional agencies and specialists whom she or he can call on if there is a crisis at a school or care facility. This includes having a list of mental health professionals as well as medical health professionals and community agencies that offer specialized services. Parents will feel relieved to know that such contacts have been established, just as they are glad to know that fire drill rules have been established and practiced. If such contacts are made prior to a possible emergency arising, then galvanizing help in a situation of acute child stress will be easier for teachers, administrators, and families.

CONCLUSIONS

Adults who work daily with children have a variety of stresses that they deal with on a daily basis, whether it is dealing with children, personnel, parents, supervisors, or other consultants and mental health professionals. Stresses can arise from unavoidable environmental problems too. In a center, a backed-up toilet can cause stress or the fact that several teachers suddenly called in sick that morning. It is important to try to reduce everyday stresses in order to avoid caregiver burnout. You are a precious resource and a specially trusted figure in the children's lives. Although caring for infants, toddlers, and young children can be hard work, physically and emotionally, it is deeply important work. This chapter provides some techniques and positive strategies for how to handle a variety of stresses in daily life as a caregiver or as an outreach worker with families.

STUDY QUESTIONS

What are some techniques to reduce stress when dealing with parents?

How can you identify troubling sexualized behaviors in children?

When do you need to seek professional supports for children?

Why is it important to create liaisons between parents and professionals?

CHAPTER 9

PERSONAL STRESS-BUSTING IDEAS FOR ADULTS CARING FOR CHILDREN

Living with others, whether in a caregiver's own family or in the world of child care, inevitably entails some frustrations and stresses. Teachers and care providers need a supply of personal ways they can decrease their own stress.

TAKE TIME FOR SELF-REFLECTION

Take time for self-reflection. Think about how you approach interpersonal hassles and problems. When you feel uptight or very mad, do you try to figure out whether the anger you feel comes from the present situation only? Does it take you back to ancient slights, mistreatments, and disappointments? When we find ourselves reacting with strong negative emotions, sometimes this is the result of a stress echoing back into our past.

A father grimly explained how he hated that his kinder-garten-age son was still thumb sucking when nervous or uncertain. The father's anger was so strong. His response was to order the child angrily to get the thumb out of the mouth. His orders were not getting the child to stop thumb sucking. Together we gently explored where this strong shame and anger might have come from. Years ago, the father's parents had scolded and shamed him for patting his genitals. His long-ago experience with shame about sensuous body activity in his own childhood was reverberating in the present way in which he chastised his own son.

We need to listen for echoes of old experiences from our own childhoods when we were shamed or chastised if we find ourselves very angry at young children's sensuous behaviors to manage their stresses. We need courage to banish these ghosts from our current ways of working to decrease young children's stress.

Let us listen to our own voice tones, feel the tenseness in our stomachs, teeth, shoulders, or other body parts. Then we can better practice breathing and other relaxation techniques. We can take fierce pride in knowing about our own selves—vulnerabilities and all. How did you handle times that you were not treated fairly? Did you keep pain inside? Did you lash out at the hurtful person? Did you bury shame deep inside you and have you avoided examining how it currently affects your interactions with young children?

Impressively, in research with young single high-school dropout mothers of infants, self-reflectivity proved a powerful catalyst for maternal change. Some of the mothers were randomly assigned to receive excellent home visitation knowledge and tips for positive emotional relationships with the baby. Others were in a control group. Regardless of whether the moms had or had not received months of expert home visitation information and support, some of the mothers had thought a lot about how they were mistreated in childhood, and they had determined to treat their own babies more lovingly. The infants of these reflective mothers were thriving better than the other babies during that first year of life (Brophy & Honig, 1999). Reflectivity is a crucial adult component to galvanize more loving interactions and less stress for children.

Reflect also on whether you are getting enough sleep. Staff burnout can result from chronic feelings of tiredness. Assess how much late-night television may be cutting down on sleep time. Search out some tried-and-true soothing readings that work for you. Keep those readings right by the bed at night to help you drift more easily into sleep.

Be mindful of where stress lodges in your body. Tune into the ways your unique self tends to express stresses. Do you have a deep frown mark between your brows? You are the best person to figure out how and where stress is hurting your daily functioning. When you are angry, do you become aware of which body muscles express stress most typically? Do you feel your throat tightening when upset or your jaw muscles clenching? You are the best person to figure out where tensions lodge in your body. As you carry out body exercises with the children in your group, you may find that relaxing muscle groups eases tensions for you as well as the children. If your shoulders ache, ask a loved one for a shoulder and back massage and give one in return.

PRACTICE BREATHING DEEPLY

When we are upset or tense, we breathe more shallowly. If someone criticizes you or says something snide or unfeeling, quietly take deep breaths through your nose. Then breathe long breaths slowly out through your mouth a few times. Do this even when you have a strong urge to lash out verbally with an indignant or sarcastic retort. Your thoughts and feelings belong to you. Upbeat thoughts and feelings are less stressful physiologically. But *actions* that ameliorate a stressful situation can indeed increase or decrease your tense feelings.

FEED YOUR BODY RIGHT

Juice and a doughnut for breakfast provide a quick sugar high, and then the blood sugar level plummets soon after. If blood sugar levels are steady, people are more likely to feel okay rather than draggy, discouraged, or irritable from being ravenously hungry at midmorning. A combination of complex carbohydrates, protein, and a little fat allows the blood sugar level to rise gradually over several hours. Start the day with a breakfast that features not only your juice and coffee but also protein such as an egg, a whole-grain cereal or bread, and a bit of butter. This will provide enough energy to cope with stresses that may arise during morning activities with children.

Sometimes seasonal affective disorder (SAD) accounts for stressed, unhappy moods during dark winter months. Maintaining a steady blood sugar level relieves these feelings. So does a good daily dosage of natural light, which increases body production of serotonin. Serotonin is a neurotransmitter essential for feeling upbeat with high energy. Center board members who help raise funds for your facility may be able to earmark some money to install full-spectrum light fixtures in your classroom.

FLING AWAY TENSIONS SYMBOLICALLY AND VISUALIZE THEM BEING SENT FAR AWAY

Private ways to decrease stress need to be part of your repertoire! In a private place, such as your bedroom at night, imagine that the stress is traveling from your toes gradually all the way up through your body and through your arms. Then fling out the stress by shaking each arm in turn outward to get rid of the anxious feelings. Visualize the tense feelings soaring away in opposite directions and traveling far from you.

TRY PROGRESSIVE MUSCLE RELAXATION

If someone puts you down and rage feelings are unleashed, clench your fist really tightly in your pocket. Breathe out and then unclench your hand. Do this a few times. This strong tensing and relaxing of a body part also gives you time to think up a good way to handle the situation without physically trying to get back at that person and getting into trouble! This exercise may already be a part of the isometrics body-relaxation techniques you are using with the children in your group.

GET RID OF OLD GRUDGES

What if harsh interactions have occurred with others in your past? You have already done lots of mourning when these difficult episodes occurred. You cannot change the person toward whom you have old grudges from long ago. But you can indeed take up the challenging work of changing your own self little by little. When trying to cope with a strong stress, you will have to climb two symbolic mountains: the mountain of sadness and also the mountain of anger/rage. Before we can get to the rich, rolling meadows of life and smell the flowers, we have to trudge both mountains to experience and get over a major stress. Keep on working at getting over both mountains—sorrow and anger.

DO NOT OBSESS ABOUT PAST SLIGHTS

Do not let ghosts of harsh past times "rent space in your mind" (Honig, 2005). Occasionally, we obsess about past slights, criticisms, betrayals, or disappointments. We think a lot about what has gone wrong in our lives rather than what we are doing right now that is positive and life affirming—especially helping young children grow and flourish in the sunshine of your nurturing care!

USE GUIDED IMAGERY

Do not let negative past interactions continue taking up space in your head. In a quiet space, perhaps with soft music in the background, practice creating images that can ease stress and get rid of tensions. Put the negative events and hurtful comments of the past in an imaginary large garbage bag. Trudge, in your imagination, to a nearby dump. Then toss the trash; let go of these burdens. You will feel free—no more crowding of negative vibes from the past in the mansions of your mind!

PRACTICE FORGIVENESS

If someone says something sarcastic and mean, smile gently at that person and walk away (Knutson, Enright, & Garbers, 2008). You might even shake your head, give a kindly smile, and then walk away. Certainly, the forgiveness smile is a special kind of mask. A mask of peaceful, purposeful maturity sometimes helps an adult sail safely through an interpersonal situation where the main inside feelings are fury, fear, and resentment. Practice putting on a *forgiveness mask* to decrease stress. Feel proud of yourself when you are able to summon feelings of forgiveness. Try to feel sorry for people who fly off the handle and say or do mean or rude things. Be really glad that your family's love, your own hard work, and sustenance from your faith community have sustained your growth into becoming a generous, loving adult. Be proud of acquiring and even hoarding a large selection of positive ways to respond to mean or rude remarks or actions! Folks who are optimistic thinkers experience better health, less stress, and more positive experiences with others in life.

When you walk away rather than yell back when another adult is temporarily out of control, then you are gracious enough to show that you therapeutically understand that the angry person just blew it and showed a lack of good impulse control. Impulse control is one of the strong goals parents and teachers strive to bolster in the children they care for! Longitudinal research has found that children who have more of this treasured ability show fewer classroom troubles in later school years and are markedly less likely to use drugs and alcohol in their teens (Wong et al., 2006).

BE CAREFUL WITH CRITICISM

Think about how we, as adults, respond if a visitor to our home acts critical. Suppose a visitor comments that our desk looks messy and piled up. Or perhaps visiting relatives comment that we should not let our kids run wild and get up from the table as soon as they want to rather than sit politely during the entire meal. Criticism wounds a person's feelings about the self. How do most folks respond to the stress of criticism? Some blow up in reactive anger. Others, if they are criticized, listen reflectively then shrug off the criticism. They keep their own views and stick to their own course of action regardless of what people feel or say. Others feel devastated. Teens have confided that they even changed the way they dress or the music they listened to if jeered at by peers. I asked a teen once to explain to me about why teenagers smoke. "It's peer pressure," she answered me instantly. "If you want your friends to like you, then you do what they think is cool!"

Some people act very defensive if criticized for a fault or a mistake. Most of us do not enjoy being criticized! But some folks sarcastically spring into a strong emotional defense of their action or lack of action. Some people are so attuned to anticipate stress that they will act *prior* to an anticipated negative event in order to forestall feeling stressed. Have you noticed that sometimes in a dating couple one person will break off the relationship *before* the feared event of being dumped by the partner in that relationship?

Cool it. Take criticism in stride. So a desk is messy. So someone else has a neater house. That is life. We need to accept and acknowledge that, given busy lives, we are doing the best we can to be loving, kind, and keep our living spaces in mostly okay shape!

GET OUT TENSIONS WITH VIGOROUS PHYSICAL ACTIVITY

When you exercise regularly, the cells lining the arteries boost their production of nitric oxide. Nitric oxide keeps the arteries smooth, widens them, and keeps them open. Exercise increases the amount of blood that is pumped through your blood vessels and stimulates bone marrow to produce new cells for the arterial lining. Increased artery flexibility slows aging, reduces the chance of inflammation of blood vessels, and reduces stress.

Physical exercise and pleasurable lovemaking are activities that signal the body to release endorphins. These chemicals brighten mood and help a person feel good. Choose your own physical work-out formula! Go for a long bike ride. Swim and splash the water with strong strokes as if slashing out the bad vibes inside you! Take a long walk and swing your arms as you stride along. Dig in the garden and plant flowers. Take up ice skating, Tae Kwan Do, or kayaking. Join a bowling team or a volleyball game in the local park. If you are carry-ing infants or toddlers, you are bending, stretching, and lifting a lot during your work day. Then you can smile and reflect that your exer-cise quota may well be included in all the daily physical work of car-ing for little children.

EXPERIENCE FLASHES OF BEAUTY

Focus for a little while every day on the awesome loveliness of a part of the world of nature around you. Even a few seconds of focus on beauty during the day can relax and expand your sense of well-being. Did you notice the flickery silver of a squirrel's tail as he nosed about in the bright green new grass your neighbor has planted on his lawn? Did a finch with buttery yellow feathers come and eat your sunflower seeds this summer? Do you look out the window at the riot of sky color as the day draws to a close? Get totally absorbed in a wondrous sunset.

Look at amazing art works in a book, at a museum, or online. Web sites reveal more than current information. We can find awesome cave drawings of ancient aurochs, horses, and deer drawn on cave walls by artists who lived over 25,000 years ago. Marvel at the way in which ancient artists used bear claw marks on caves to enhance their carvings of shaggy fur on the bison they carved on cave walls.

Go to an aquarium and watch fish, dolphins, and sea anemones. Stand breathless and become absorbed in front of an exhibit of the "bal-let performances" of tiny jellyfish that float in their tanks with effortless grace and clouds of drifting tentacles.

Notice the delicious dimples on each fat little fist as you kiss a baby's fingers and he gurgles and stretches forth his fingers so that you can pretend to nibble lovingly on them again. Find beauty for every season to delight your soul. Go to a rose garden and sniff the subtle scents of roses. Watch Monarch butterflies on their great migrations southward in the autumn. Their jewel-colored wings slowly open and close as they feast on a flower in the sunshine of an early autumn morning.

During the winter, force some paper-white narcissus and hyacinth bulbs in a glass bowl filled with pebbles and water. You and the children can inhale with deep pleasure the gorgeous fragrance that fills your room. Each season provides experiences of beauty. The vivid red of a newly fallen leaf startles with its glorious color even as it is about to shrivel and die! The bark of a tree shimmers with a velvety chocolate color after a soaking rain. A child's face lights up as you share an admiring comment or a tender word with him. There are zillions of snowflakes. Awesomely, each snowflake is unique on the windowpane decorated by Jack Frost. A rainbow spans the sky and you interrupt a lesson to go to the window with all the children and rejoice in the splendor of its great arc across the sky.

APPRECIATE THE SMALL AND BIG KINDNESSES OF THE YOUNG CHILDREN YOU CARE FOR

In addition to nature and our physical environment, there are plenty of opportunities to enjoy beautiful gestures from the children you are teaching. A child does something loving with a peer, and the beauty of that generous gesture fills your soul.

> Willy did not want to go to a special tutoring time with the adult who had come to take him out of class. He threw himself on the floor crying. Seeing his distress, Ofira put out a comforting hand. She lay down and put her cheek next to his and said, "Willy, don't cry. It's okay. I will go with you. We'll ask the teacher if we can go together."
>
> Jonas explained with concern to his mom that Otis, his chess pal in an afterschool activity, was being teased and touched inappropriately on the school bus. His mother quietly asked what he thought he might be able to do to make things better. "Mom, I decided he could sit by the window and I sit near the aisle in the bus. That way, nobody can mess with him and he is safe."

Such living embodiments of kindness before your eyes flash as an inward beauty of a child's soul.

READ POETRY; WRITE POETRY

Poetry moves us with its rich language and awesome power of breathtaking imagery. Poetry can reverberate and soothe an aching sadness or conjure wondrous and noble feelings. Writing poetry about stressful feelings is often a great relief. One teacher had to return the foster child she had nurtured so lovingly for nearly 2 years to other care. The toddler went back into what, alas, continued to be an abusive, chaotic family situation. The teacher attempted to visit, but the toddler turned away from her in despair. The child responded with rejection as if she had been abandoned by this adult whom she had begun to trust. The teacher found that writing poetry about her grief helped relieve some of the deep anguish she felt.

KEEP A JOURNAL

Writing their reflections in a journal, teachers sometimes get sudden insights about possible solutions to stressors in the classroom. Writing descriptions of upsetting situations may give the distancing perspective that allows a broader picture of what happened prior to an upsetting episode and what could have been done to avoid the difficult explosion that happened, for example, when two children were struggling angrily over the same desired toy.

A journal helps us process uncertain, angry, bitter feelings or mark joyful events in our lives. Journaling assists us in developing a habit of noticing our own feelings—whether happy or unhappy. Journal writing over many months can reveal to us how we are progressing at healing old feelings of resentment or trying new ways to cope with personal problems. Journaling helps us write down personal goals as well as our dreams and wishes for our future. Especially, journaling allows us to write down *what we are thankful for* specifically week after week. One home visitor reported that after a year of visiting a very suspicious mom, the window shades were open when she arrived at the apartment. Her journal reflected her thankfulness at this sign of growing trust between the mom and herself and renewed her dedication to working with this fragile family to resolve some of their difficult issues.

TALK WITH A FRIEND

Getting bad feelings off your chest is such a relief. Find a friend who lets you *kvetch*, someone to whom you can confide worries and annoyances and share exasperating times in your life. Choose a friend whom you can trust not to share your confidences with others. Choose someone who is genuinely concerned with your well-being. Stress is relieved when we complain and talk about our stresses with a sympathetic and warmly empathetic, caring friend. This unburdening feels like a special healing potion. It takes the festering poison out of one's spirit, just as Androcles took the poison thorn out of the lion's paw in the fable we know from so long ago. Self compassion comes easier when we talk with a friend.

Social, intimate support lowers stress. Cuddle with a spouse. Attend a faith service with others, where prayers, music, and friendly people help participants unwind—without leaving folks with a hangover, the result of other short-term palliatives like drinking bouts.

CARRY OUT AN ACTIVITY THAT MAKES YOU FEEL PERSONALLY COMPETENT

Bake a pie. Repair a broken step on your porch. Knit an afghan for a hospital program for newborns from low-income families. Paint and freshen up a room in your apartment. Glue that broken piece of pottery you have waited so long to repair. Scrub the kitchen floor. Buy the new shirt that goes terrifically with other clothes in your closet. Go fishing and broil your own caught fish for dinner. You may be steaming inside and ruminating about something nasty or worrisome that someone said or did. As you do something to show you are in charge of your life, you make good things happen in your life space, and you will feel less upset.

LET GO OF BEING A PERFECTIONIST

No person can ever be perfect. Some days things just go awry. A toilet in the center overflows. A few children have diarrhea. A parent calls and complains harshly to a teacher. The toddlers cannot seem to settle into sleep. If we accept that life has some difficult days, some wonderful days, and some just-ordinary times, then we will be less anxious when some days seem to fill up with more stresses than other days.

FIND WAYS TO PLAY IN YOUR OWN LIFE

Play relieves stress. You know yourself best. What kind of play helps you unwind? Do you have friends to go out for dinner with, go bowling with, play ping-pong with, shoot baskets with, or just sit around and schmooze together? Find a neighbor with whom you enjoy an early morning run or a swim. Share awful and groan-able puns in e-mail messages with friends. Do you enjoy Scrabble, Sudoku, Mancala, Go, or solving cross-word puzzles? Do you have a friend you can walk in the woods with in the autumn and just kick piles of leaves about as you talk together? A playful attitude keeps burnout at bay!

TREASURE MUSIC AS A THERAPY TOOL TO CALM TENSIONS

Music, for millennia, has soothed upset folks. King Saul, when in turbulent and violent moods, would ask young David to play his harp to calm the king's dark moods.

Play soothing music, even sentimental music, to unwind body tensions. Listen to your favorite albums or songs. Sing along as you do chores when you get home in the evening. Sing in the shower. Sing aloud in the car as you drive to and from work. Do not worry about sounding like an opera star. Few of us have perfect pitch, but all of us can enjoy some kind of music. Music soothes and magically makes our worries and our annoyances float away on the sounds of our favorite pieces (Honig, 1995).

WATCH OLD COMEDY VIDEOS

Deep belly laughs lower all those stress chemicals coursing through the body of an adult who has had a difficult and tense day. Check out some old comedy videos from the local library's collection. Decades later, we can still burst into laughter watching the oldies. We grin at the outrageous behaviors of the Three Stooges, W. C. Fields, or Groucho Marx with his brothers. Who among us can ever forget the antics of Abbott and Costello's comic baseball routine, "Who's on first"? Watching old comedies relieves tensions and helps decrease stresses from daily hassles.

COMMIT RANDOM ACTS OF KINDNESS

One of the more satisfying ways to help yourself feel like a good person in this world, despite life's troubles and exasperations, is to do good deeds, little *random acts of kindness!* This is easier if you practice AL—active listening—to the message of a person's body in interaction with others or the environment. One evening, walking by an apartment building, I saw two girls playing a jumping game on the house steps. Standing nearby quietly, the mom looked weary, sad, and lonely. Pausing briefly to smile at the parent, I remarked, "The girls sure love to jump and they are so good at it! Isn't it amazing how much life energy kids have? You sure have beautiful children!" She raised her head, straightened her shoulders, and smiled.

REFRAME RESPONSES TO EASE STRESS

As we become aware that a child may have had stressful infant–parent interactions whose consequences are reenacted in bullying or victim social relations in the classroom, we are better able to handle our own angry responses. We are more clearly able to choose and use a technique to tame the dragon of anger (Eastman & Rozen, 1994). Anger rings alarm bells in each of us. Anger alarms dredge up ancient echoes of when adults were very mad at us when we were kids. Reframing gives us a breather. If we realize how a given distressful behavior came about in the classroom, we can think more clearly and choose a technique to defuse the stressful situation. Help an irritated adult to see a problem in another light—as adventurousness or interest rather than naughtiness. A teacher was calling all the preschoolers to a table for snack time. Dexter ignored her. He was watching in fascination as the teacher's aide squeezed a soapy sponge with water and cleaned off the table where they had just been playing with clay. How he wanted to squeeze the sponge and help with cleanup! But the teacher reacted as if the child was deliberately not listening to her call to come right away for snack time. Reframing can decrease teacher stress.

Sometimes you can help an adult become consciously aware that there are worse problems and stresses than the current one. Suppose you see a father dragging a youngster along the street hurriedly. The dad might be frowning, thinking that his child is just being stubborn, not trying to keep up the pace. You smile and remark cheerfully, "Well it sure is hard for a kid's little legs to keep up with a daddy's strong long legs!"

Perhaps while at the playground, you notice a parent is getting exasperated while trying hard to keep up with the toddler who is bent on venturing all over the playground. Time after time the toddler resists being dragged back to sit on a bench. Remark with a loving smile to the parent at the park: "You have such a handsome little child. What a wonderful *adventurer* your toddler is. He wants to explore the whole world!"

HONE YOUR ACTIVE LISTENING SKILLS

With AL you may more successfully help some folks understand young children's motivations with gentle positive, brief comments. Of course, sometimes AL needs to be extended further. A tired toddler was yowling as Mom dragged her from the mall toward the exit. "She sure looks like she wants to be picked up and carried," I remarked sympathetically and smiled at Mom. "I wish someone would pick *me* up and carry me," retorted Mom! Her remark required another AL comment reflecting empathy for the stressed adult who has to cope with the difficulty of going out shopping with a tired, tiny child.

Outside a community center in snowy Syracuse, a father was nagging his young son about playing "angels in the snow." Over and over the young boy threw himself against the banks of snow piled up on either side of the cleared pathway to the center door. He was making an impression of his own body on the packed snow pile. The father was warning the child to stop and threatening that mom would be very upset and scold if the boy's snowsuit got soaking wet. I smiled at the stranger, and remarked in a calm tone, "We don't have any wonderful Florida sand up north to make sand castles or patterns with our bodies. We sure do have lots of snow for children who just love to play 'angels in the snow' with tall snow piles. And thank goodness for our trusty washers and dryers!" The father looked at me for a moment. Then, as if a light bulb went on, he smiled. He turned to his son and in a cheerful voice said, "Go ahead. You can make angels in the snow as much as you want. We can dry your snowsuit easily in the dryer if we need to later on."

NURTURE A PERSON YOU KNOW WHO HAS SORROWS AND WOES

When we help others, we often feel more competent and more satisfied with ourselves even if we ourselves feel quite stressed by our current life situation. If you have a family member who is going through a rough patch in life, such as a divorce or job loss, invite them over on a weekend evening for popcorn and a game of Scrabble or cards. As we make others feel better, we feel a surge of moral and emotional empowerment that lifts our own spirits and decreases our stresses.

Hospitality helps reduce stress, as reported in an ad in *Newsweek* affirming the importance of hospitality at Hilton Hotels (Hilton Hotels, 2006):

> Studies done at the University of Michigan, Bowling Green State University, and elsewhere suggest[ed] that people who volunteer appear to lower their risk for heart disease, diabetes, and other cardiovascular diseases. Other benefits that researchers have identified include improved memory and reduced heartburn, headaches, colds, and insomnia. One study concluded "helper's high" reduced stress and released endorphins, the body's natural painkillers, much as exercise does (with less sweat!). (p. 67)

Invite an older or ill uncle or aunt to have coffee and home-baked pie with you on a weekend afternoon. Offer to drive an older person who is afraid to drive at night to a night concert you are going to attend anyway. When you know that a friend has been homebound with a sick child for days, call to find out how that friend is doing and express your caring feelings. If your friends are e-mail fans, you can share outrageous puns and absurd jokes through e-mail. Even if you do not have time to type a friendly message, the e-mail joke sharing is a way to say, "I am thinking about you. You are a special person in my life."

EMBODY PEACEFULNESS IN YOUR INTERACTIONS

Children who are stressed need their special adults to be there as figures of strength, security, protection, and peacefulness. Yes, our first action when faced with distressed and distressful behaviors is to think about what the child might be feeling. Is his angry response a way to defend his play construction from a child who wants to knock it down? Is he acting out angry feelings because at home he feels badgered and jeered at by a sibling? Is his fearfulness about joining in at circle time reflective of a shy temperament? Does the child need bodily soothing, more one-on-one time with teacher, slower introduction with more explanatory reassurances in order to ease him into new activities? Our thinking and wondering skills come first. Our insights as *child development detectives* into problems children display are essential. They permit us to choose the interaction tools that can ease each individual child's distress and lead to decreased classroom stress.

Paley (1990) generously has shared her insights as a classroom teacher constantly learning from the children in her care. She writes of

> The essential loneliness of each child. Our classrooms, at all levels, must look more like happy families and secure homes, the kind in which all family members can tell their private stories, knowing they will be listened to with affection and respect. (p. 148)

SEEK OUT RESOURCES

Teachers can count on many resources, written and audiovisual, as well as other providers and the children themselves, to help shed light on some child stresses and to offer ideas that may work to calm or solve some problems. One resource may be articles available at exchangeeveryday@ccie.com, an e-mail site. A daily e-mail stress buster resource for adults is provided by Elizabeth Scott at stress. guide@about.com, the site of the About Stress Management newsletter. To learn more about how to help traumatized children with disturbing behaviors, the Child Trauma Academy and Dr. Perry offer articles on the e-mail site ctanewsletter@aol.com. Some books deal with the spectrum of mental health issues for children (Greenspan & Wieder, 2006). Some books address specific child stresses, such as separation anxiety (Balaban, 2006), toddler behavioral contradictions (Lieberman, 1993), and aggression (Tureski, 1985). Some books support teacher attempts to enhance the emotional climate of the classroom (Baker & Manfredi-Petit, 2004; Hyson, 2006). Some books address fears and grief more specifically to help children and their caring adults to cope (Robinson, Rotter, Robinson, Fey, & Vogel, 2005; Walz & Kirkman, 2005). Also important are scholarly books that bring us up to date on new techniques that therapists are using to help children with specific mental health issues, such as reactive attachment disorder (Berlin, Ziv, Amaya-Jackson, & Greenberg, 2007).

As noted in Chapter 7, a rich array of books is available to read with young children to help them learn about coping with *specific* stresses such as adoption (Blomquist & Blomquist, 1990) or to learn about managing a variety of emotional feelings (Conlin & Friedman, 1986). Use books to gain ideas to spark group discussions that lead children to create their own insightful understandings of stresses and how they might better cope with them.

KEEP YOUR JOY PIPES OPEN

Children know how to cry, rage, and express anger and disappointment. But they also teach us what real joy looks like. With eyes sparkling and bodies loose and free, they run and skip and twirl. They dance to music, giggle, and chase each other happily on the playground. They respond with shrieks of delight to puppet shows; they come running and shouting to show us the treasure they find—a fall leaf with brilliant red colors they spied on the ground. They clutch a droopy dandelion picked triumphantly from a grassy yard as a present to give Mom when they get home.

CONCLUSIONS

In addition to insightfulness as we interpret children's stress signs and respond in ways to restore harmony, adults also need to choose and use stress-reducers that work for us in our own lives. Whether we do yoga, reduce stimulants (e.g., cut down on too many cups of coffee), practice forgiveness and compassion, or use music to soothe our own stresses, we can then more effectively serve as a model and a beacon of peacefulness for the children. Even though some of our children come to child care or school burdened with pressures and woes, caregivers can indeed ease those stresses in their unique, perceptive, and loving relationship with each child.

A teacher needs faith, knowledge, wisdom, and supports in the long process of assisting children to become enthusiastic learners. But teachers also deeply need to engage themselves in intimate interactions that will ensure the development of empathic, emotionally secure young persons able to get along harmoniously with classmates and adults as they grow toward maturity. Children have their *joy pipes* open, despite distresses in their lives. Adults need to inspect their joy pipes from time to time. Adults tend to let their joy pipes get clogged with fatigue, anger, impatience, and worries.

Remember that scientists have reported that positive moral and empathetic responses are strongly built into our human ways of responding just as much as they have noted the human possibility for negative responses (Pinker, 2008). So give yourself permission to feel hopeful despite frustrations with some children's difficulties.

Give yourself opportunities in the midst of everyday chores and business to rejoice. Maybe on a walk in the park the children heard a frog noisily calling out and watched him jump and plop into the pond. Maybe the children shouted with joy and pointed as they finally spotted the red cardinal who had been singing away up in a tree. Touch joy from time to time in your own life as well as when life goes well with the children you serve.

STUDY QUESTIONS

Why is it important to take time for self-reflection?

How can you use guided imagery to release stress?

What are some ways you can experience the beauty of nature in your daily life to reduce stress?

How can keeping a journal or reading and writing poetry reduce stress?

REFERENCES

Ainsworth, M.D.S. (1973). The development of infant-mother attachment. In B.M. Caldwell & H.N. Ricciuti (Eds.), *Review of child development research* (Vol. 3). Chicago, IL: University of Chicago Press.

Ainsworth, M.D.S., Bell, M.B.V., & Stayton, D.J. (1971). Individual differences in the strange situational behavior of one-year-olds. In H.R. Schaffer (Ed.), *The origin of human social relations*. London: Academic Press.

Andersen, L.B., Harro, M., Sardinha, L.B.B., Froberg, K., Eklund, U., Brage, S., et al. (2006, July). Physical activity and clustered cardiovascular risk in children: A cross-sectional study (The European Youth Heart Study). *The Lancet, 368* (9532), 299–304.

Ayoub, C., Grace, P., & Neuberger, C.M. (1990). Working with maltreated children and families in day care settings. In S.S. Cherazi (Ed.), *Psychosocial issues in day care*. Washington, DC: American Psychiatric Press.

Baker, A.C., & Manfredi-Petit, L.A. (2004). *Relationships, the heart of quality care: Creating community among adults in early care settings*. Washington, DC: National Association for the Education of Young Children.

Balaban, N. (2006). *Everyday goodbyes. Starting school and early care: A guide to the separation process*. New York: Teachers College Press.

Baum. F. (2000). *The wonderful wizard of Oz*. New York: Harper Collins. (Original work published 1900).

Baumrind, D. (1971). Harmonious parents and their preschool children. *Developmental Psychology, 41,* 92–102.

Bergen, D. (2006). Play as a context for humor development. In D.P. Fromberg & D. Bergen (Eds.), *Play from birth to twelve: Contexts, perspectives, and meanings* (2nd ed.) (pp. 141–156). New York: Routledge.

Berlin, L.J., Ziv, Y., Amaya-Jackson, L., & Greenberg, M.T. (2007). *Enhancing early attachments*. New York: Guilford Press.

Bessell, H., & Palomares, U. (1970). *Methods in human development: Theory manual*. San Diego, CA: Human Development Training Institute.

Blomquist, G.M., & Blomquist, P.B. (1990). *Zachary's new home. A story for fostered and adopted children*. New York: Imagination Press.

Bloom, G.E., Cheney, B.D., & Snoddy, J.E. (1986). *Stress in childhood: An intervention model for teachers and other professionals*. NY: Teachers College Press.

Bornstein, M., Hahn, C., Gist, N.F., & Haynes, O.M. (2006). Long-term cumulative effects of childcare on children's mental development and socioemotional adjustment in a non-risk sample: The moderating effects of gender. *Early Child Development and Care, 170* (2), 129–156.

Bowlby J. (1969). *Attachment*. Volume 1 in *Attachment and loss*. New York: Basic Books.

Bowlby J. (1989). *Attachment. Secure and insecure attachment*. New York: Basic Books.

Brett, D. (1986). *Annie stories: For parents of children troubled by divorce, nightmares, death, a new baby, starting school and other fears*. Victoria, Australia: Penguin Books.

149

Brophy, H.E., & Honig, A.S. (1999). Reflectivity: Key ingredient in positive adolescent parenting. *The Journal of Primary Prevention, 19* (3), 241–250.

Butterworth, N. (1996). *The hedgehog's balloon.* London: Harper Collins.

Carson, J. (1992). *You hold me and I'll hold you.* New York: Orchard Books.

Cauthen, N.K., & Fass, S. (2008). *Measuring income and poverty in the United States.* New York: National Center for Children in Poverty, Columbia University, Mailman School of Public Health.

Cheney, K. (2006, September/October). Living longer. *AARP Bulletin,* 66–69, 93.

Child Care Lounge site. (September, 2006). http://www.childcarelounge.com/articles/stress.htm

Clifton, L. (1975). *My brother fine with me.* Austin, TX: Holt, Rhinehart & Winston.

Conlin, S., & Friedman, S.L. (1986). *Ellie's day. Let's talk about feelings.* Seattle, WA: Parenting Press.

Cosby, B. (1997). *Little Bill: The meanest things to say.* New York: Scholastic Press.

Crary, E. (2001). *Willy's noisy sister.* Seattle, WA: Parenting Press.

Daniels, H. (Ed.). (2005). *An introduction to Vygotsky* (2nd ed.). London: Psychology Press.

Deffenbacher, J.L. (1995). Ideal treatment package for adults with anger disorders. In H. Kassinove (Ed.), *Anger disorders: Definition, diagnosis, and treatment* (pp. 151–172). Washington, DC: Taylor & Francis.

Denny, S., Clark, T.C., Fleming, T., & Wall, M. (2004). Emotional resilience: Risk and protective factors for depression among alternative education students in New Zealand. *American Journal of Orthopsychiatry, 74* (2), 137–149.

dePaola. T. (1981). *Now one foot, now the other.* New York: G.P.'s Putnam Sons.

Dickenson, E. (2006). Play in early childhood helps stunted children. E-mail abstract from the *British Medical Journal.* Contact: edickinson@bmj.com.

Dudley, M. (1947). *Bad mousie.* Chicago, IL: Children's Press.

Eastman, M., & Rozen, S.C. (1994). *Taming the dragon of anger in your child: Solutions for breaking the cycle of family anger.* New York: John Wiley & Sons.

Eliker, J., Noppe, I.C., Noppe, L.D , & Fortner-Wood, C. (1997). The parent-caregiver relationship scale: Rounding out the relationship system in infant/child care. *Early Education and Development, 8* (1), 83–100.

Elkind, D. (1981). *The hurried child.* Reading, MA: Addison-Wesley.

Erikson, E.H. (1950). *Childhood and society.* New York: Norton.

Essa, E., Favre, K., Thweatt, G., & Waugh, S. (1999). Continuity of care for infants and toddlers. *Early Child Development and Care, 148,* 11–19.

Ewing, A.R., & Taylor, A.R. (2009). The role of child gender and ethnicity in teacher-child relationship quality and children's behavioral adjustment in preschool. *Early Childhood Research Quarterly, 24,* 92–105.

Feindler, E. (1995). Ideal treatment package for children and adolescents with anger disorder. In H. Kassinove (Ed.), *Anger disorders: Definition, diagnosis, and treatment* (pp. 173–195). Washington, DC: Taylor & Francis.

Fiese, B. (2006). Who took my hot sauce? Regulating emotion in the context of family routines and rituals. In D.K. Snyder, J.A. Simpson, & J.N. Hughes (Eds.), *Emotional regulation in couples and families: Pathways to dysfunction and health* (pp. 269–290). Washington, DC: American Psychological Association.

Fink, R. (2006). *Why Jane and John couldn't read and how they learned.* Newark, DE: International Reading Association.

Freud, S. (1935). *A general introduction to psychoanalysis.* New York: Liveright.

Furman, E. (1974). *A child's parent dies.* New Haven, CT: Yale University Press.

Garbarino, J. (2008). *Children and the dark side of human experience: Confronting global realities and rethinking child development.* New York: Springer.

Garbarino, J., & DeLara, E. (Eds.). (2002). *And words can hurt forever: How to protect adolescents from bullying harassment, and emotional violence.* New York: Free Press.

Gillespie, L.G. (2006). Cultivating good relationships with families can make hard times easier! *Young Children, 61* (5), 53–55.

Gilman, P. (1992). *Something from nothing.* New York: Scholastic Press.

Goldstein, A.P. (2000). *The Prepare Curriculum: Teaching prosocial competencies.* Champaign, IL: Research Press.

Goleman, D. (2006). *Social intelligence.* New York: Bantam Books.

Gordon, S. (1983). *Girls are girls and boys are boys: So what's the difference?* Fayetteville, NY: Ed-U Press.

Gordon, S., & Gordon, J. (1974a). *A better safe than sorry book.* Fayetteville, NY: Ed-U Press.

Gordon, S., & Gordon, J. (1974b). *Did the sun shine when you were born?* Fayetteville, NY: Ed-U Press.

Gordon, T. (1970, 2000). *Parent effectiveness training: The proven program for raising responsible children.* New York: Three Rivers Press.

Graceffo, S. (2006, September 13–20). Life lessons: Research indicates that troubled childhoods could lead to gullible behavior. *Syracuse New Times,* p. 34.

Grahame, K. (1983). *The reluctant dragon.* New York: Henry Holt.

Greenspan, S.I. (2006, March). Working with the child who is sensory reactive. *Scholastic Early Childhood Today, 20* (5), 22–23.

Greenspan, S.I., & Wieder, S. (2006). *Infant and early childhood mental health: A comprehensive developmental approach to assessment and intervention.* Washington, DC: American Psychiatric Publishing.

Haus, N. (2006, September). Caring. *In Good Health,* pp. 1, 32.

Havill, J. (1989). *Jamaica tag-along.* Boston: Houghton-Mifflin.

Hilton Hotels. (2006, July 2–10). The power of hospitality. *Newsweek,* p. 67.

Hoban, R. (1994). *Best friends for Frances.* New York: Harper Collins.

Honig, A.S. (1979) *Parent involvement in early childhood education.* Washington, DC: National Association for the Education of Young Children.

Honig, A.S. (1982a). *Playtime learning games.* Syracuse, NY: Syracuse University Press.

Honig, A.S. (1982b). Research in review: Prosocial development in children. *Young Children, 37* (5), 51–62.

Honig, A.S. (1986a). Research in review: Stress and coping in children. *Young Children,* Part 1: *41* (4), 50–63; Part 2: *41* (5), 47–59. Reprinted in J.B. McCracken (Ed.), *Reducing stress in young children's lives.* Washington, DC: National Association for the Education of Young Children.

Honig, A.S. (1986b). *Risk factors in infancy.* London: Gordon & Breach Science Publishers.

Honig, A.S. (1988). Research in review: Humor development in children. *Young Children, 43* (4), 60–73.

Honig, A.S. (1993). Toilet learning. *Day Care and Early Education, 21* (1), 6–9.

Honig, A.S. (1995). Singing with infants and toddlers. *Young Children, 50* (5), 72–78.

Honig, A.S. (1996). *Behavior guidance for infants and toddlers.* Little Rock, AR: Southern Early Childhood Association.

Honig, A.S. (1997). Infant temperament and personality: What do we need to know? *Montessori Life, 9* (3), 18–21.

Honig, A.S. (1999). Creating a prosocial curriculum. *Montessori Life, 11* (2), 37–39.

Honig, A.S. (2000). Psychosexual developments in infants and young children. Implications for caregivers. *Young Children, 55* (5), 70–77.

Honig, A.S. (2001). Promoting creativity, giftedness, and talent in young children in preschool and school situations. In M. Bloom & T.P. Gullotta (Eds), *Promoting creativity across the life span* (pp. 83–126). Washington, DC: Child Welfare League of America.

Honig, A.S. (2002). *Secure relationships: Nurturing infant/toddler attachment in early care settings.* Washington, DC: National Association for the Education of Young Children.

Honig, A.S. (2003a). Bringing up a book lover. *Scholastic Parent and Child, 10* (5), 32–33.

Honig, A.S. (2003b). How teachers and caregivers can help young children become more prosocial. In E. Chesebrough, P. King, T. Gullotta, & M. Bloom (Eds.), *A blueprint for the promotion of prosocial behavior in early childhood* (pp. 51–91). New York: Kluwer Publishers.

Honig, A.S. (2004a). Don't let anyone rent space in your head. [Review of C.M. Dalpiaz. *Breaking free, starting over: Parenting in the aftermath of family violence.*]. *PsycCritiques, 49,* Supplement 7. (http://www.psychinfo.com/psycCritiques/display).

Honig, A.S. (2004b). Raising happy achieving children in the new millennium. In K.L. Freiberg (Ed.), *Annual editions: Human development* (Article 20, pp. 94–110).

Honig, A.S. (2005). The language of lullabies. *Young Children, 60* (5), 30–36.

Honig, A.S. (2006). Sociocultural influences on gender-role behaviors in children's play. In D.P. Fromberg & D. Bergen (Eds.), *Play from birth to twelve: Contexts, perspectives, and meanings* (2nd ed.) (pp. 378–393). New York: Routledge.

Honig, A.S. (2008). Understanding and working with non-compliant and aggressive young children. *Early Child Development and Care, 178* (7 & 8), 665–687.

Honig, A.S. (2009). Stress and young children. In E. Essa & M. M. Burnham (Eds), *Informing our practice: Useful research on young children's development* (pp. 71–88). Washington DC: National Association for the Education of Young Children.

Honig, A.S., Kim, Y., Ray, K., & Yang, H.J. (2006). *Teacher education and soothing strategies with infants and toddlers.* Poster session presented at the Early Head Start Research Conference, Washington, DC.

Honig, A.S., & Pollack, B. (1990). Effects of a brief intervention program to promote prosocial behaviors in young children. *Early Education and Development, 1,* 438–444.

Honig, A.S., & Wittmer, D.S. (1992). *Prosocial development in children: Caring, sharing, and cooperation: A bibliographic resource guide.* New York: Garland Press.

Howes, C. (1999). Attachment relationships in the context of multiple caregivers. In J. Cassidy, & P.R. Shaver (Eds.), *Handbook of attachment theory and research* (pp. 671–687). New York: Guilford Press.

Hughes, S. (1989). *Dogger.* London, UC: Collins.

Hyson, M. (1979, July). Lobster on the sidewalk: Understanding and helping children with fears. *Young Children, 34* (5), 54–60.

Hyson, M. (2006). *The emotional development of young children. Building an emotion-centered curriculum* (2nd ed.). New York: Teachers College Press.

Jalongo, M.R. (2003). *Early childhood language arts* (3rd ed.). New York: Pearson Education Group.

Kaiser, B., & Rasminsky, J.S. (2003). *Challenging behavior in young children. Understanding, preventing, and responding effectively.* Boston, MA: Allyn & Bacon.

Kline, S. (1985). *Don't touch!* Niles, IL: Albert Whitman and Company.

Knutson, J., Enright, R., & Garbers, B. (2008). Validating the developmental pathway of foregiveness. *Journal of Counseling & Development, 86 (2),* 193–199.

Kobak, D. (1979). Teaching children to care. *Children Today, 8* (6–7, 34–35).

Koplow, L. (1996). *Unsmiling faces: How preschools can heal.* New York: Teachers College Press.

Kucuker, S. (2006). The family-focused early intervention programme: Evaluation of parental stress and depression. *Early Childhood and Care, 176* (3&4), 329–241.

Ladd, G.W. (2006). Peer rejection, aggressive or withdrawn behavior, and psychological maladjustment from ages 5 to 12: An examination of four predictive models. *Child Development, 77* (4), 822–846.

Lally, R.J., Mangione, P., & Honig, A.S. (1988). The Syracuse University Family Development Research program: Long-range impact of an early intervention with low-income children and their families. In D. Powell (Eds.), *Parent education as early childhood intervention: Emerging directions in theory, research, and practice* (pp. 79–104). Norwood, NY: Ablex Publishers.

Langford, P.E. (2005). *Vygotsky's developmental and educational psychology.* London: Psychology Press.

Leboyer, F. (1976). *Loving hands.* New York: Alfred A. Knopf.

Levine, J. (2004). *Responding to young children's fears.* http://www.childcarelounge.com/articles/fear.htm

Lewis, C.S. (1994). *The chronicles of Narnia.* New York: Harper Collins. (Original work published 1956).

Lewis, M. (2006, September 24). The ballad of big Mike. *New York Times Magazine,* 38–47, 112, 114–115.

Lewis, S. (1989). *One-minute Jewish stories.* New York: Dell Publishing.

Lieberman, A.F. (1993). *The emotional life of the toddler.* New York: Free Press.

Lines, D. (2008). *The bullies: Understanding bullies and bullying.* London: Jessica Kingsley Publishers.

Main, M., & Solomon, J. (1986). Discovery of an insecure, disorganized/disoriented attachment pattern: Procedures, findings, and implications for the classification of behavior. In M. Yogman & T.B. Brazelton (Eds.), *Affective development in infancy.* Norwood, NJ: Ablex.

Marquardt, E. (2005). *Between two worlds: The inner lives of children of divorce.* New York: Crown.

Martin, C.L. (1981). *The myth of masculinity.* Cambridge, MA: MIT Press.

McCain B.R. (2001). *Nobody knew what to do: A story about bullying.* Morton Grove, IL: Albert Whitman & Company.

McEwen, B. (2002). *The end of stress as we know it.* Washington, DC: National Academies Press.

McGinnis, E., & Goldstein, A.P. (1990). *Skill-streaming in early childhood: Teaching prosocial skills to the preschool and kindergarten child.* Champaign, IL: Research Press.

Metzger, S. (1998). *Dinofours: It's beach day.* New York: Scholastic Press.

Morales, J.R., & Guerra, N.A. (2006, July/August). Effects of multiple context and cumulative stress on urban children's adjustment in elementary school. *Child Development, 77* (4), 907–923.

Myers, P., & Nance, D. (1986). *The upset book: A guide for dealing with upset people.* South Bend, IN: Academic Publications.

National Institute of Child Health and Human Development-ECCRN. (2001). Childcare and family predictors of preschool attachment and stability from infancy. *Developmental Psychology, 37,* 847–862.

National Institute of Child Health and Human Develepment-ECCRN. (2006). *Child care and child development: Results from the NICHD study of early child care and youth development.* New York: Guilford Press.

Orpinas, P., & Horne, A.M. (2006). *Bullying prevention: Creating a positive school climate and developing social competence.* Washington, DC: American Psychological Association.

Paley, V. (1990). *You can't say you can't play.* Cambridge, MA: Harvard University Press.

Papalia, D.E., & Olds, S.W. (1995). *Human development* (6th ed.). New York: McGraw-Hill.

Paulson, J. (1997). Active peacemaking in the Montessori classroom. *Montessori Life, 10* (1), 42–43.

Perry, B.D. (1993, Summer). Neurodevelopment and the neurophysiology of trauma 11: Clinical work along the alarm-fear-terror continuum. *The Advisor, 6* (2), pp. 1, 14–19.

Perry, B.D. (1994). Neurobiological sequelae of childhood trauma: Post-traumatic stress disorder in children. In M. Murberg (Ed.), *Catecholamines in post-traumatic stress disorder: Emerging concepts* (pp. 253–276). Washington, DC: American Psychiatric Association Press.

Perry, B.D. (1999). Memories of fear: How the brain stores and retrieves physiologic states, feelings, behaviors, and thoughts from traumatic events. In J. Goodwin & R. Attias (Eds.), *Splintered reflections: Images of the body in trauma* (pp. 26–47). New York: Basic Books.

Perry, B.D. (2002). Childhood experience and the expression of genetic potential: What childhood neglect tells us about nature and nurture. *Brain and Mind, (3)*, 79–100.

Pinker, S. (2008, January 11). The moral instinct. *New York Times Magazine Section,* pp. 32–38, 51, 55–57.

Piper, W. (1997). *The little engine that could.* Uhrichsville, OH: Barbour.

Prelutsky, J. (1982). *The sheriff of Rottenshot.* New York: Mulberry Paperback.

Quan, V., & Wien, C.A. (2006). The visible empathy of infants and toddlers. *Young Children, 62,* 22–29.

Rheingold, H.L, & Hay, D.F. (1976). Sharing in the second year of life. *Child Development, 47,* 1148–1158.

Robertson, A. (1982). *Day care and children's responsiveness to adults.* In E. Zigler & E. Gordon (Eds.), *Day care: Scientific and policy issues.* Boston: Auburn House.

Robinson, E.H., Rotter, J.C., Robinson, S.L., Fey, M.A., & Vogel, J. (2005). *Fear, stress, and trauma: Helping children cope.* Austin, TX: PRO-ED.

Rogers, F., & Sherapan, H. (n.d.). *What do you do with the mad that you feel?* (VHS tape #8011 for multimedia training kit plus activity book #7011). Washington, DC: National Association for the Education of Young Children.

Roizen, M.F., & Oz, M.C. (2006, November). Is stress making you fat? *Reader's Digest,* 128–34.

Ruppin, D. (2006, Fall). Searching for home. *Na'Amat Woman,* 4–7, 26.

Rutter, M. (1996). Stress research: Accomplishments and tasks ahead. In R.J. Haggerty, & L.R. Sherrod (Eds.), *Stress, risk, and resilience in children and adolescents: Processes, mechanisms, and interventions* (pp. 384–385). New York: Cambridge University Press.

Sendak, M. (2003). *Where the wild things are.* New York: Harper Collins (original work published 1963).

Selye, H. (1982). History and present status of the stress concept. In L. Goldberger & S. Breznitz (Eds.), *Handbook of stress: Theoretical and clinical aspects.* New York: Free Press.

Seuss, D. (1954). *Horton hatches an egg*. New York: Random House.

Seuss, D. (1955). *The king's stilts*. New York: Random House.

Seuss, D. (1956). *Horton hears a who*. New York: Random House.

Shure, M. (1992). *I can problem solve: An interpersonal cognitive problem-solving program (preschoolers)*. Champaign, IL: Research Press.

Shure, M. (1994). *Raising a thinking child*. New York: Holt.

Shure, M., & Spivack, G. (1978). *Problem-solving techniques in childrearing*. San Francisco, CA: Jossey-Bass.

Sigel, I. E., & Saunders, R. (1979). An inquiry into inquiry: Question asking as an instructional model. In L. Katz (Ed.) *Current topics in early childhood education,* (vol. 2), p. 169–193. Norwood, NJ: Ablex.

Simon, N. (1974). *I was so mad*. Niles, IL: Albert Whitman & Company.

Simon, N. (1981). *Nobody's perfect, not even my mother*. Niles, IL: Albert Whitman Company.

Snyder, D.K., Simpson, J.A., & Hughes, J.N. (2006). *Emotional regulation in couples and families: Pathways to dysfunction and health*. Washington, DC: American Psychological Association.

Sroufe, L.A., & Fleeson, D. (1988). Attachment and the construction of relationships. In W.W. Hartup & Z. Rubin, *Relationships and development* (pp. 51–71). Hillsdale, NJ: Erlbaum.

Stevenson, R.L. (1924). *A child's garden of verses*. Akron, OH: Saalfield Publishing Company.

St. George, D. (2008, October 5). Study: Activities enrich children, don't stress them. *The Syracuse Post Standard,* pp. A10–11.

Syracuse University. (2006, September 5). Mindfulness based stress reduction. *The Syracuse Record,* p. 7.

Thomas, A., Chess, S., & Birch, H.G. (1968). *Temperament and behavior disorders*. New York: New York University Press.

Tureski, S. (1985). *The difficult child*. New York: Bantam Books.

Viorst, J. (1976). *Alexander and the terrible, horrible, no good, very bad day*. New York: Atheneum.

Vygotsky, L. (1978). *Mind in society: The development of higher psychological processes*. Cambridge, MA: Harvard University Press.

Wachter, O. (1983). *No more secrets for me*. Boston: Little, Brown.

Wallerstein, J.S. (1987). Children of divorce: Report of a ten-year follow-up of early latency-age children. *American Journal of Orthopsychiatry, 57* (2), 199–211.

Wallerstein, J., Lewis, J., & Blakeslee, S. (2000). *The unexpected legacy of divorce*. New York: Hyperion.

Walt Disney Productions. (1986). *Hiawatha's kind heart*. New York: Bantam.

Walz, G.R., & Kirkman, C.J. (2005). *Helping people cope with tragedy and grief*. Austin, TX: PRO-ED.

Welsh, R. (1976). Violence and the overpunished child. *Journal of Pediatric Psychology, 1,* 68–71.

Werner, E.E., & Smith, R.S. (1992). *Overcoming the odds: High risk children from birth to adulthood*. Ithaca, NY: Cornell University Press.

WestEd, Center for Child and Family Studies. (undated). *Flexible, fearful or feisty* [Motion picture]. Sacramento, CA: California Department of Education.

Wittmer, D.S., & Honig, A.S. (1988). Teacher re-creation of negative interactions with toddlers. In A.S. Honig (Ed.), Optimizing early childcare and education (Special Issue). *Early Child Development and Care, 33,* 77–88.

Wolfson-Steinberger, L. (2000). "Teacher! He hit me!" "She pushed me!"— Where does it start? How can it stop? *Young Children, 55* (3), 38–42.

Wong, M.M., Nigg, J.T., Zucker, K.A., Puttler, L.I., Fitzgerald, H.E., Jester, J.M., et al. (2006, July/August). Behavioral control and resiliency in the onset of alcohol and illicit drug use: A prospective study from preschool to adolescence. *Child Development, 77* (4), 1016–1033.

Xu, Y. (2006). Toddlers' emotional reactions to separation from their primary caregivers: Successful home-school transition. *Early Child Development and Care, 176* (6), 661–674.

Zins J.E., Elias, M.J., & Maher, C.A. (Eds.). (2007). *Bullying, victimization, and peer harassment: A handbook of prevention and intervention.* New York: Haworth Press.

CHILDREN'S BOOK BIBLIOGRAPHY

Baum, F. (2000). *The wonderful wizard of Oz.* New York: Harper Collins. (Original work published 1900)

Butterworth, N. (1996). *The hedgehog's balloon.* London: Harper Collins.

Carson, J. (1992). *You hold me and I'll hold you.* New York: Orchard Books.

Clifton, L. (1975). *My brother fine with me.* Austin, TX: Holt, Rinehart & Winston.

Cosby, B. (1997). *Little Bill: The meanest things to say.* New York: Scholastic Press.

Crary, E. (2001). *Willy's noisy sister.* Seattle, WA: Parenting Press.

dePaola, T. (1981). *Now one foot, now the other.* New York: G.P. Putnam's Sons.

Gilman, P. (1992). *Something from nothing.* New York: Scholastic Press.

Grahame, K. (1983). *The reluctant dragon.* New York: Henry Holt.

Havill, J. (1989). *Jamaica tag-along.* Boston: Houghton-Mifflin.

Hoban, R. (1994). *Best friends for Frances.* New York: Harper Collins.

Hughes, S. (1989). *Dogger.* London: Collins.

Kline, S. (1985). *Don't touch!* Niles, IL: Albert Whitman and Company.

Lasker, J. (1980). *Nick joins in.* Chicago, IL: Albert Whitman and Company.

Lewis, C.S. (1994). *The chronicles of Narnia.* New York: Harper Collins. (Original work published 1956)

Lewis, S. (1989). *One-minute Jewish stories.* New York: Dell Publishing.

Metzger, S. (1998). *Dinofours: It's beach day.* New York: Scholastic Press.

Piper, W. (1997). *The little engine that could.* Uhrichsville, OH: Barbour. (Original work published 1920)

Prelutsky, J. (1982). *The sheriff of Rottenshot.* New York: Mulberry Paperback.

Sendak, M. (2003). *Where the wild things are.* New York: Harper Collins. (Original work published 1963)

Simon, N. (1974). *I was so mad.* Niles, IL: Albert Whitman & Company.

Simon, N. (1981). *Nobody's perfect, not even my mother.* Niles, IL: Albert Whitman Company.

Stevenson, R.L. (1924). *A child's garden of verses.* Akron, OH: Saalfield Publishing Company.

Seuss, D. (1954). *Horton hatches an egg.* New York: Random House.

Seuss, D. (1955). *The king's stilts.* New York: Random House.

Seuss, D. (1956). *Horton hears a who.* New York: Random House.

Viorst, J. (1976). *Alexander and the terrible horribile, no good, very bad day.* New York: Atheneum.

Walt Disney Production. (1986). *Hiawatha's kind heart.* New York: Bantam.

INTERNET RESOURCES

Anti-Gossip and Anti-Bullying Board Games: http://www.jistlife.com

Child Care Lounge: http://www.childcarelounge.com/articles/stress.htm

Child Trauma Academy: http://www.childtrauma.org/

Daily Stress-Buster Guides: stress.guide@about.com

Get Out the Mad Cookies Recipe: http://pbskids.org/rogers/parentsteachers/theme/1691.html

Stress Management Board Games: http://portal.creativetherapystore.com/portal/page?_pageid=94,54628&_dad=portal&_schema=PORTAL

Stress Management Cognitive-Behavioral Program: www.creativetherapystore.com

Stress Management General Information: http://stress.about.com

INDEX

Tables and figures are indicated by *t* or *f* respectively.